simple
STONESCAPING

simple
STONESCAPING

Gardens, Walls, Paths & Waterfalls

PHILLIP RAINES

Sterling Publishing Co., Inc.
New York

Prolific Impressions Production Staff:

Editor in Chief: Mickey Baskett
Copy Editor: Phyllis Mueller
Graphics: Dianne Miller, Karen Turpin
Photography: Jerry Mucklow, Phillip Raines
Administration: Jim Baskett

Library of Congress Cataloging-in-Publication Data Available

10 9 8 7 6 5 4 3 2

Published by Sterling Publishing Company, Inc.
387 Park Avenue South, New York, N.Y. 10016

Produced by Prolific Impressions, Inc.
160 South Candler St., Decatur, GA 30030

© 2002 by Prolific Impressions, Inc.

Distributed in Canada by Sterling Publishing
c/o Canadian Manda Group, One Atlantic Avenue, Suite 105
Toronto, Ontario, Canada M6K 3E7
Distributed in Great Britain by Chrysalia Books
64 Brewery Road, London N7 9NT, England
Distributed in Australia by Capricorn Link (Australia) Pty. Ltd.
P.O. Box 704, Winsor, NSW 2756 Australia

Printed in China
Sterling ISBN 0-8069-2761-5

Acknowledgements

First, I wish to thank Phyllis Mueller, who turned me on to the opportunity to do this book even after editing my articles and knowing my tendency to write poetry when I should be writing recipes. I also thank Mickey Baskett for developing faith in me and allowing me to ramble and digress about details.

I'd like to thank Bo Bradshaw for the apprenticeship and for turning his business over to me at such an early age and Bob Williams for working with me – his experience, strength, and true grit have gotten me out of a lot of jams in jobs that were over my head. He sees more with one eye than I ever will with two.

I'm truly indebted to Jon Rembert, my next door neighbor, for doing a perfect size project for a homeowner and insisting that it not look like a mason did it, though it's some of the best work I've ever seen. I'm also thankful to his wife Lisa for inspiring and encouraging him and never resenting my stopping by unannounced.

My deepest thanks to Jim Long and Amy Hayes, who asked me to do the perfect stone project for the book. Thanks to my friend and fellow saxophonist Amy Lee for allowing herself to be photographed as she worked on her own stonescape.

I wish to fully express my appreciation to Chuck Clark – architect, designer, cartographer, and extraordinary quick draw draftsman. Through collaboration and suggestion, he has taught me more about the nature of design than anyone should learn without paying handsomely for it. Time will recognize his brilliance.

The fullest appreciation is gladly expressed to Rodney Clemons and Rice & Clemons Gardens and their gracious clients for allowing us to photograph all the beautiful water features and stone arrangements.

I appreciate Randy, Darlene, and all the folks at Fieldstone Center for having such a well-stocked stoneyard and for providing such courteous service. I am also thankful to Bob Paul at Eagle Granite in Elberton, Georgia for the gracious tour of the quarry and fabrication shop. I am particularly thankful to Steve Milsap for introducing me to Bob and taking me on a field trip to the abandoned quarries and showing me where he picks up free stone scrap. Steve is truly an inspiration as an artist, sculptor and musician. I hope one of his talents makes him wealthy one day because his work is as good as any I have seen.

I am indebted to all my apprentices but especially to Lynn Attwool for his British wit and for carrying on the torch of the trade even though he became my competition. I am most inspired by Steve Whatley, my star apprentice. His young muscles saved my-worn-out ones and his courage and calm insight made me truly believe in him. Thanks to Eric Bohling at the Kings Masons for hiring Steve when I didn't have any work and showing him tricks I needed to know. And to Alan Vennes, who left Wall Street to become a stone mason at an age most when most masons retire. You made the right choice.

Thanks to The Brick Institute (particularly Bill Kjorlean, truly the nicest guy in the hard surfaces trades) for the chance to lecture to the trade and for believing in me as an artist and a craftsman. And to Craig Nelson, a chimney sweep who shared a career's worth of work with me as a collaborator and friend. And to all the guys at the Brew House for listening and telling me about their work, especially Bill, my new old friend whose stories of the bygone days of masons and how they worked constantly fascinate me. Thanks even to Ross Westcott, who knows I should be better.

Finally, I wish to thank my sons, Will and Luke, for maturing me and my wife, Kathy, for enduring me. Typing Kathy's thesis on hydration and cognitive learning explained a lot about stone and the body, but she is my hero for other reasons.

About the Author
Phillip Raines

Phillip Raines has been a mason and contractor for over 25 years, working in the Atlanta area. He has designed and built patios and walls of stone, brick, and block and worked with homeowners and masons of all walks of life. His ornamental Victorian chimneys have received national attention and have been awarded for excellence in design and construction from the Brick Institute of America. He led the Brick Mural Team to complete three municipal sculptures for Underground Atlanta, including the Brick Train. He lectures at masonry conferences and chimney sweep conventions on chimney construction and has carved several fireplaces out of unfired brick.

Raines also is a working saxophone player in reggae and wedding bands. When he's not at his treehouse on a river in Florida, he works and lives in the historic district of downtown Decatur, Georgia with his wife of 25 years, his two teenage sons, and a big lazy dog named Ben.

Contents

DESIGN

"I can't build it until you design it."
Anonymous existentialist tradesman

Stone is an enduring narrative that can explain a culture's understanding of nature. Stonehenge is the most noted stone "clock," though other cultures, long vanished, erected similar monuments. The designer of a stonescape can play with the heavens and use stone to create a narrative. The placement of large leaning boulders can split shafts of sunlight and make a sundial on a lawn or through a kitchen window. Columns can be placed to center the location of the northern star and used as a reference to the zodiac.

The Japanese use stones in gardens to represent mountains and give the illusion of expansive spaces in small gardens. By determining lines of perspective to a vanishing point from a primary point of view, boulders of varying heights can be placed that exaggerate distances. Inspiration for this type of design can be gleaned from studying Oriental watercolors or books on Oriental gardens, which take great pains to explain proper stone placement. Like lines pulling the corners of a net, stone can enclose the themes of a garden with threads of certainty and substance.

Peering out into a space and seeing what isn't there – but could be – is the beginning of design. As with a blank page or canvas, the possibilities of a stonescape are limitless. Conceiving an overall plan for a garden ultimately involves visualizing each component separately and then looking at how each part affects all the other parts. Stone solutions may be as functional as a retaining wall or as frivolous as placing boulders to create the illusion of a mountain vista.

The existing features of the yard guide layout, and the functions of managing water and terracing slope determine placement. The stone adds the beauty; selecting the type and color you prefer satisfies the very subjective determination of what looks good.

Designing a project that is within the physical and fiscal scope of a do-it-yourselfer requires understanding what lies behind the finished outcome. A small project like a sitting wall, 50 feet long, 2 feet thick, and 2 feet high is within the capabilities of any able-bodied person. Any design can be altered to encompass work that is realistic, manageable, and a true pleasure.

Conventional Design Approach

The conventional approach is to measure the space and the existing elements, then draw the plan to scale. To get accurate bids, scale drawings are indispensable. A contractor will use drawings to calculate the time and materials required. Architects, landscape architects, engineers, and contractors can be engaged in the design process; if you're on a tight timetable, collaboration is essential.

New digital tools, such as landscape software with click-and-drag boulders and trees, make the process more accessible than ever to non-professionals.

ABOUT THIS BOOK

A neighbor who had renovated her house over the past 15 years was tackling the final frontier, her backyard. Tying together her plans was a material of proven beauty and endurance – stone.

She had done her homework. Her next door neighbor, an architect, had measured her backyard with her and drawn it to scale. He located and placed the pool, the surrounding decking, and areas to sit and enjoy the yard. I saw the word "stone" in several places with arrows to indicate areas of paving bordered with planters and retaining walls. I asked, "What type of stone are you planning to use?" She turned to me and said, "You don't have a book with a bunch of pictures of different kinds of stonework, do you?"

It was a simple question, but as I thought of all the books I had, I realized each one included only a few examples, usually limited to the author's work or the publisher's preference. Books written by landscape contractors favored drystacked walls. Historic restoration masons showed methods too expensive for the average homeowner. Some books showcased the highly engineered approaches typical of commercial construction projects. I didn't have anything that represented the mason's approach to general residential stonework to show her. Now I do, and this is it.

This book is a narrative of what I've learned about masonry. I promised my friends I would include things in the book they could actually use, and that I wouldn't be superficial. Though stonework is mostly physical, I have written about the mental aspects as well, like design, staging, and layout. You can learn all you need to learn about the physical aspects when you actually work with stone. Then the words quiet down. I've put tons of tips and theory in the text; I hope you will want to read it like a story (but you can zero in on specific topics by looking them up in the index).

The most important mental aspect of this whole book is this: Stonework is possible for anyone who has the desire to do it. It's not too heavy if you select smaller stone. It's not too exhausting if you stop when you get tired. (So much bad work comes from working after your mind and body tell you to quit.) Slowing down from the pace of the modern-day world is a great thing about the physical labor of stonework. It quiets the mind and gives a deep, lasting satisfaction like nothing else. Using stone can be simple for willing hands.

With brick and stone, I've built plenty of enduring relics; ironically, perhaps, being able to pass along the intangible aspects of the work – the tips and tricks I've learned – holds a greater value for me than the works themselves. As I write, I wonder what this book will inspire. Will you take up the trade, do a small project in your yard, or hire a mason to carry out your stone dreams? Though I explain methods of construction for the intrepid do-it-yourselfer, it is also my intention that this book can help you communicate with your mason or designer to turn your stone ideas into completed projects.

The Gradual Design Approach

All designs change as a project proceeds. A slow, do-it-yourself approach allows the design to naturally evolve. Some of the best revelations occur as you work on a project, then back off a little. See how the work affects the panorama. Make it up as you go along.

Stonework can be as peaceful and uncomplicated as gardening and still provide endless satisfaction. Stone can be gathered from your own property or ordered and delivered from a stoneyard and put in place as an ongoing project, a little at a time.

Think Before You Work

Forethought and planning can reduce toil. "Form follows function" may be a cliche, but it speaks volumes. A stone retaining wall, for example, will fall if it doesn't follow the tried and true rule of thumb that the thickness of the wall at the base must be half the wall's height. (More about walls in Chapters 8 and 9.) Simplifying a design – reducing the height of the wall, for example – will save time, money, materials, and (oh, yes) toil.

Ambitious projects take true grit to see them through. The work is hard. (One surly laborer I hired (briefly) said, "This is prison work.") Viewing a completed project is liberating. It is a triumph of will.

A total renovation of the room without a roof – the backyard – may need to be coordinated through collaboration: A surveyor to draw the yard, a grading contractor to slope and haul away dirt, a foundation contractor to form and pour footings and backing walls, and finally a stone mason to staff the project with a labor force able to complete the work in a timely fashion. If the kind of stonework you want requires equipment and experience to do it right the first time, hire a contractor. If a smaller stone job can't be strung out for a long time, hire a reputable mason.

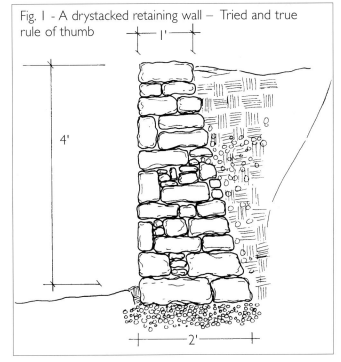

Fig. 1 - A drystacked retaining wall – Tried and true rule of thumb

1'

4'

2'

LAYOUT

Deciding where stonework will be placed can be simple or remarkably complicated. Scale drawings showing the placement of proposed features of the yard with sketches of elevations of details are the tools of the designer's craft. For most backyard projects, usually only the simplest scaled plan is necessary (and I have seen plenty of backyard renovations with no drawn plan at all).

If a designer has a knack for visualizing a completed project, the challenge then is to express that vision to the homeowner. Similarly, a homeowner can have a vision of a project but not know how to express it. The idea may be as simple as a retaining wall in front of a house at the sidewalk, say as long as your property is wide and about 4 feet high. Considerations arise even with such a simple undertaking. The exact property lines as stipulated in a deed survey should be referenced. Neighborhood covenants may prohibit alterations of property as viewed from the street. The smaller the project, the less these issues come into play.

To avoid conflict, consider all the possible restrictions as you develop your plan. Check with the building department of your municipality to see if the work you're planning requires a permit. Call the local utilities, particularly if you are planning to dig near the street. It's free and can save you countless problems. Just driving a wooden stake could cut communications for an entire neighborhood, and there's always the danger of hitting a gas line.

Laying out your ideas on the existing terrain with markers like a garden hose and flags can help develop a workable plan.

A woman I know placed marker flags all over her backyard to mark the placement of the walls she wanted to build and photographed them with her digital camera. She printed the picture with her inkjet printer and drew the walls on the print with colored pencils to make a very believable perspective elevation drawing – by simply connecting the marker flags.

LAYOUT TOOLS

A retractable tape and some kind of marking device are the tools of the first step of layout.

• Measuring Tape

I use a 100-ft. cloth tape for measuring, the type used for track and field events. Cloth tapes are more flexible on curves and stay where you put them. Metal tapes tend to snag and bind, and eventually they rust – plus they're never long enough for garden layouts (but they are useful for general measuring once the job is underway).

• Marker Flags & Stakes

I prefer wire **marker flags**, the type utilities use to mark for digging. They can be inserted in dirt with less effort than **wooden stakes**, which require a hammer to set and are more difficult to remove. Marker flags cost pennies and come in bundles at building supply stores.

Using a garden hose to lay out a curved wall.

Children love marker flags. I once laid out posts for a shed with marker flags. I even ran diagonal measurements to verify that the shape was square. As I turned my back for just a minute to get my posthole digger, my four-year-old son gathered up the flags. He waved them like a spectator in a 4th of July parade, presented them to me proudly, and said, "Daddy, you left these." If there is any advantage to hammering in grade stakes it is that you can usually find the holes the stakes made. The wire used for marker flags leaves practically no trace in the soil. An arrow or circle painted on the soil showing the location of the flag can help you find where you put them in case they are moved.

• Hose

My favorite tool for plotting irregular shapes is a 50-ft. **garden hose**. It stays put, even on hills, and adjusts with a kick here and there to get those subtle undulations so favored for flowing, curvy walls and walkways.

• Marker Paint

Marker flags, hose, and stakes are good for visualizing the placement of elements of a stonescape, but they all have to be removed when digging begins. Before removing them, mark their locations on the soil with spray **marker paint**. The container can operate upside down and can be accessorized with a device that holds the can close to the ground and has a trigger mechanism on the handle. Marker paint will endure a hard rain. I keep three colors of marker paint on hand – green for the first layout, blue on my second guess, and white when I'm sure. I tell laborers to dig to the white lines and ignore the other colors.

• Other Kinds of Markers

Before marker paint, a digging line might have been marked with **sand**, garden **lime**, or **cornmeal** or scratched in the dirt with a stick. Of course, none of these methods is impervious to water.

I use **sidewalk chalk** to mark on buildings and hard surfaces like concrete and stone. All markings eventually disappear as digging and the foot traffic of work begins.

FINDING GRADE

Referencing measurements to a permanent feature, like the corner of the house or a tree will help relocate them once you have broken ground. This point of reference is called the benchmark.

I place a benchmark at a height of 5 feet to aim the crosshairs of my **builder's level**. Builder's levels are relatively inexpensive to rent and are the most accurate way to determine heights of future walls and the grading if the terrain is going to be altered.

Alternatives to a builder's level are less accurate and slower but less expensive. A **line level** is hooked over a length of string in the center of the span, and the string's height is adjusted on stakes where the string is tied. The stakes should be sturdy so the string can be pulled tight. Once the level is determined, I mark the string's location on the stake with a pencil and lower the string. With a pocketknife, I cut a V-shaped notch on the stake for the string to slide into and to keep the string from slipping.

A very accurate way to determine grade is with a **water level**, which is a piece of clear plastic tubing 3/8" in diameter and about 30 feet long. This simple, highly accurate device is inexpensive and, unlike a builder's level, can place level points around corners and obstructions. Its origins are unclear, but it's speculated that hollow reeds sealed with pitch were used for leveling the pyramids.

A less accurate way to attempt to level an area is with a 4-ft. level taped or clamped to a straight 2x4 and wooden stakes. This is fine for short spans. It is slightly more accurate to mark the stakes with a pencil than to level the stakes by pounding them with a hammer. Relying on marks on a stake instead of the top of the stake works for form boards for footings or for benchmarks for grade strings.

DRAWING A PLAN TO SCALE

> *"An accurate scale drawing can only be made when the job is finished."*
> Anonymous realistic architect

For complex projects, scale drawings are essential. Even if changes are made in the process of developing a design, making changes on paper with an eraser is much easier than chiseling apart stonework. For a do-it-yourselfer, grid paper is best for plotting out your plan. You can designate each square on the grid paper to be a foot or two and count the squares to determine your dimensions.

If your yard is large, you might have a surveyor measure and draw it for you. (This usually costs a few hundred dollars.) The surveyor will include sewer lines and underground utilities, accurate borders and easements for the property, and the locations of trees and their drip lines. (The drip lines shows the farthest perimeter of a tree's branches, which is believed to be the perimeter of the tree's vital roots.) Using this survey as a template allows you to easily sketch new features of a stonescape on tracing paper.

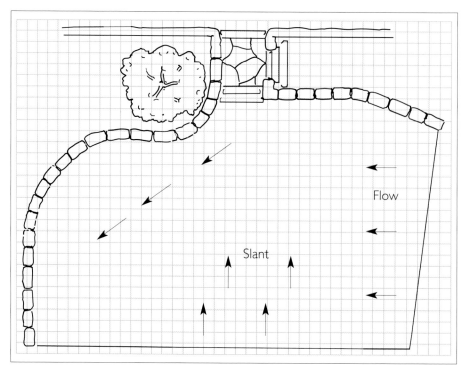

A scale drawing with arrows indicating drainage. The wall was designed around the dripline of the tree.

□ = 1'0"

16

ELEVATIONS & SECTIONS

If plans are the footprint of a project, **elevations** are the face. Features like gate entrances are illustrated in elevations to show height and shape. (For an example, see the chapter on columns.) Instead of elevations, a designer may make notations on a plan like *TOW 4'4"*. (TOW stands for "top of wall.")

Sections illustrate a "cut" through the wall or structure to show the profile or vertical reinforcement inside. Elevations and sections are illustrated in two dimensions and don't imply perspective.

DRAINAGE

> *"A planner's first job is to manage water."*
> Chuck Clark, architect and planner

Water flows downhill. This simple truth must be considered in all aspects of design because only fire is more destructive to a home than water. Water can saturate the soil around a foundation and cause settling, which will, in turn, move walls and make roofs sag. Water in the soil promotes pests of all kinds and breeds molds and fungus. Directing water away from a house is a design function of primary importance. I have repaired stone columns on porches that failed only because of bad gutters and downspouts.

Drainage for Walls

The force of water is a threat to a masonry wall no matter how strong the wall is; water that slowly flows through the soil will push on a retaining wall and must be released. A well-engineered

Above: Drain box, surface drain trough with covers, corrugated pipe, drain intersection.

Left: Weep holes allow water to trickle out the face of the wall, relieving pressure. This granite wall with beaded mortar joints has rectangular weep holes. Gutter downspouts were used to form the holes. In a veneered wall, weep holes are installed as the block is laid, using common smooth PVC pipe (the type used for plumbing drain lines).

Drainage (cont.)

wall considers this hydraulic action. Drystacked walls allow water to flow through the spaces between the stones. Gravel behind a wall allows water to disperse. Weep holes – openings in the base of a mortared wall that are backed with gravel – give water a directed path for escape. **French drains** course water away from the back of a wall; they consist of pipes (usually black corrugated plastic, 6" in diameter) with holes or slots at the top. Gravel laid on top of the holes blocks soil but not water, which trickles into the pipe and is carried away. The higher the bank of dirt behind a retaining wall, the more crucial drainage becomes.

Drainage for Paving

A backyard that slopes towards the house can become the opportunity to build something beautiful – nothing inspires the need for stone retaining walls more. Add proper grading and a stone patio, and the problem is solved.

Large paved areas may have multiple slopes and drain collection points. Before paving begins, drain boxes are located and trenches are dug for drainpipes. The paving is sloped to the drain boxes, which collect water and are connected to drainpipes, and the edges of the patio. Multiple slopes, determined with string and stakes, create subtle valleys and ridges that divide the water into smaller areas and reduce the overall runoff for each area. Cement is handy as a base to level drainpipes and can stabilize collection boxes. Placing cement on top of drainpipes prevents later settling of paving that spans the pipes and their trenches.

Water pooling on stonework accelerates deterioration by saturating the stone, making it susceptible to freezing and delaminating. Puddles also collect silt, which can cause slick spots and an environment favorable to molds, mosses, and fungi. For safety, it is crucial to have proper sloping for drainage on steps.

There are fewer problems with water when paving joints are filled with gravel, granite dust, or soil than with joints filled with mortar, but a high volume of flowing water will wash away joints and bedding. In places like these, paving should be mortared.

AESTHETICS

Regardless of the approach to laying stone, the methods of composition in stonework are the same. Ian Cramb, the best mason to write a book on stone methods (his trowel is in the Smithsonian), describes composition as the beauty of function.

Stones in a wall are like faces in a crowd – each has a story. By studying the stone selection and placement of old stone structures, patterns can be revealed that not only hold the wall together structurally, but can also please the eye in the same way artfully arranged flowers do.

Right: A chimney of rounded stones.

Above: A stone bridge was formed by placing stones over a metal drainpipe that was topped with cement.

Left: A stone chard sculpture.

chapter 2

About Stone

"Rocks, and lots of 'em. That's what we have here."
Farmer overheard talking to his mule

Throughout the earth (and other heavenly bodies as well) stones are practically everywhere. A field may be – as the saying goes – "lousy with stone," requiring removal of the stone before planting or other work can begin. To farmers, stones are a nuisance. The picturesque stone walls that line country roads in rural areas were not built for beauty alone – they are stabilized stacks of our ancestors' unwanted refuse. In ancient times, the Roman legions included soldiers who doubled as masons. As they marched through

A stone wall borders a pasture.

Great Britain establishing forts in the farthest reaches of their empire, they paved roads with local stone and built walls to hold back the ravaging hordes.

Stone has never been easier to buy than it is now. With a phone call and a credit card, stone can be delivered right where you want to build something. Type, color, shape, and size can be easily chosen to fit your needs. Over time, the earth continuously pushes stones from the soil. A surprising number of them are ready to build with as they emerge, and many are free for the gathering.

Types of Stone

Geologists divide stone into categories based on how the stone was formed. As schoolchildren are taught, there are only a few major categories of stone:

• Igneous Stone

This type of stone is formed through volcanic action. **Granite** is an igneous rock that was lava that cooled slowly under the earth's surface. It is favored worldwide for its durability as a building material and comes in a broad spectrum of colors. Tools and techniques have been developed to work granite into an endless number of shapes. It can be polished to a reflective lapidary finish for countertops and memorials. Waving a torch over the reflective surface of granite will produce a matte finish. With some effort, granite can be cut with a sledgehammer, a hammer, and chisel, or it can be sawn with blades studded with industrial diamonds. Granite is mostly composed of mica, quartz, feldspar, and potash. It is crushed into gravel (the most popular size in construction is #57, used as aggregate in concrete and as drainage fill behind walls) and granite dust, the best underlayment for mortarless paving and a substitute for sand in mortar for granite wall construction. The dust and gravel are combined to make crusher run, used for paving roadways. Unlike gravel alone, crusher run forms a relatively impermeable surface.

• Sedimentary Stone

This stone is formed from particles settling. **Limestone** is a sedimentary rock that at one time was billions of tiny seashells that settled together. Limestone has been the mason's favorite for eons. It is much easier to work than granite because it is dense and softer. Its slightly varied colors are caused by different mineral deposits, and it is often riddled with fossils. Most **fieldstone** is sedimentary and can be split in layers. It often has mosses and lichens growing on it (which are unfortunately destroyed when they come in contact with portland-based mortar) and is stained by soil and mold spores, tannin from leaves, and airborne sap. **Sandstone** is another sedimentary stone popular for building. It is the easiest to shape, but is less durable than limestone and far less durable than granite.

• Metamorphous Stone

This type of stone has gone through a transformation due to heat and compressive stresses. **Marble** is metamorphosed limestone, **gneiss** is metamorphosed granite, and **slate** is metamorphosed clay and shale. **Quartzite** is metamorphosed sandstone that is more dense and durable than its predecessor. Geologists differ on whether to categorize stones shaped by water as metamorphosed. A rounded river slick is decidedly different than fieldstone of the same composition, if only aesthetically.

BUYING STONE

The geology behind the formation of stone is less important for the purposes of building than how it looks. Stone at a stoneyard is usually categorized by its color, its likely use, or the area where it originates. If, for example, you call a stoneyard and ask for a metamorphic stone with a high feldspar content, you would most likely be put on hold. But ask for a stone with a deep, dark color, not rounded, about 8" square and 4" thick for a garden wall, and the salesperson will tell you if some is in stock. He or she will then recommend that you visit the stoneyard and have a look for yourself.

Continued on next page

Caged stone stacked on pallets.

Fieldstone in wire fence cage.

Buying Stone (cont.)

Getting stone from a stoneyard is the easiest way to supply your project, and visiting a stoneyard is a wonderful field trip. With the dimensions of your project in hand, the sales staff can help you calculate the quantity of stone you will need and recommend quantities of sand and mortar for the project. Building stone is shipped all over the world. Labor costs, fabrication facilities, and modern shipping containers have effectively leveled the playing field for stone supply. In Atlanta, for example, jade green creek rock from Mexico for paths costs about the same as rounded white marble stones from north Georgia. Granite cobblestones from India are surprisingly cheaper than cobblestones from Vermont or Georgia.

Fieldstone is gathered today the same way it has always been gathered – it is picked up and carried. In the old days, a masonry crew would gather stone for part of the year, stockpiling it for upcoming work. These days, a gathering crew walks behind a truck and tosses the stone in the bed or piles them up in a central location. Later, the stone is placed on a pallet with a wire fence cage for shipping to a stoneyard.

Sometimes the truck will drive down a creek while the gatherers wade and collect rounded stones. For the heaviest stones, which sell for more, gatherers use a wench on the end of the truck and have a tripod and pulleys to lift the stones and put them on a stone sled. They wench the stone sled up the hill and into the truck bed.

Stone gatherers generally don't advertise to the public – they sell to wholesalers and stoneyards. Farmers, local suppliers, or builders may be able to provide leads to gathering operations or small quarries.

Quarried stone can sometimes be bought directly from the quarry at a fraction of the cost of buying it from a stoneyard. Approaching a quarry for rubble must be done with great care so as not to suggest the quarry will be put to any trouble for the favor of your picking through scraps. Quarried stone may fissure (break or split) into irregular shapes that will need to be dressed (chiseled) for building walls, but the savings are worth it for a do-it-yourselfer willing to provide the labor of picking and loading the stone.

Buying Dimensioned Stone

I often recommend clients use dimensioned stone – stone slabs cut with a saw – for special applications such as coping stones. The weathered, old look of fieldstone or river stone is sacrificed, but dimensioned accents are not unharmonious with rough work.

"Cubic stock" stone from all over the world can be ordered for capstones or cornerstones and cut to your specifications at a

Dimensioned (cut) stone stacked at a stoneyard.

A saw with a diamond blade cuts stone slabs at a fabrication shop.

A slab placed on a cutting table for chiseling at a fabrication shop.

stoneyard's fabrication shop with hydraulic splitters. Memorial (tombstone) shops also have this equipment and will fabricate (cut) pieces to your shop drawings. Stone fabricators usually have drafters who can take a rough sketch and do a shop drawing that can be fabricated.

Be advised that it can take months to fill orders, and you may be required to pay part or all of the expense up front to reserve a place in the shop's production schedule. Dimensioned stone pieces are delivered in boxes filled with excelsior or stacked on pallets.

How Much Do You Need?

The amount of stone you will need can be estimated by measuring the lengths and heights of the walls in a project and multiplying to yield the square footage of the surface stone. Knowing the thickness of the wall as well will yield the cubic footage, which can be used to calculate the total quantity of materials.

Always buy or gather more stone than you think you'll need. Learning how to shape stones will destroy a large number of them or render them useless. It takes a lot of detachment to find a stone, carry it to the truck, and get it home, just to watch it crack to pieces as you're trying to take off that last little corner for a just right fit. Even if you carefully select stone with a plan in mind, you will end up with stone you just can't use. Gather a few thousand stones, cut a few thousand stones, set a few thousand stones, and you can get pretty good at it all. At some point in your proficiency it becomes a career more than an avocation, since it takes so much time.

A machine called a guillotine cuts stone slabs.

A mason's truck loaded with sand pulls a trailer loaded with caged stone on pallets.

Above: Stone delivered by a front-end loader through a narrow driveway.

Dimensioned stone is unloaded off a trailer at the sidewalk. Workers guide the placement of the stone onto a wooden pallet.

23

GATHERING STONE

A Ride in the Country

The mason I apprenticed with was putting a room on his 1910 Craftsman bungalow and wanted the addition to match the original beaded granite foundation. The granite at the local stoneyard was too new looking, so he decided to use surface granite that was already stained and weathered.

I rode with him way out in the country, over roads that wound through fields and rolled over granite outcroppings that erupted through thin layers of grass and lichen. As we bounced over the rough terrain we faintly heard the unmistakable sound of a distant jackhammer. We followed the sound until we saw a lone man cleaving stone. We spoke with him about the size and color of stone we were looking for, and the quarryman pointed to a pile of stone to look through. It only took us a few minutes to load on a ton of material, selecting the darkest, most weathered slabs we could lift.

On the outskirts of cities, where farmland is being transformed into subdivisions and strip malls, the grading and clearing of land can reveal unwanted stone that diminishes the value of fill dirt or increases the tonnage of trucking away the dirt. Soil brokers scramble to find a place to put this by-product of construction and usually are happy to let stone be carried away.

Gathering stone is hard work that generates ingenuity in anyone left with the task. Finding stone at the top of a hill and rolling it down to the road is, of course, better than dragging it up a hill. Ramps or 2x10 planks can be used as an incline to "walk" a heavy stone into a truck.

Sometimes in a stone fabricator's scrap pile you can find flawed carved stones that are discarded, like chipped coping stone or even ecclesiastic details like stone angels with mauled faces or column capitals with damaged scrolls. This trash can be your treasure. If the scraps are not taken away, the fabrication shop will have to pay to have the scrap pile hauled to a dump or covered with fill dirt, so a scavenger is doing the shop owner a favor by clearing up space. (Naturally, **always** ask permission.)

Scavenging stone from ruins is another source for inexpensive or free materials. A drystacked stone chimney standing alone in a field, the home it once heated long gone, can yield up to 20 tons of stone if taken apart. The chimney can be tied to a truck bumper with a *long* rope and pulled down – the dramatic thud will break apart the bonded stones. An abandoned foundation or a wall buried by vines can yield collections of stones that come with their own narrative of time and place. Taking apart old stonework is a good way to learn methods of masonry.

All land belongs to someone, and permission must be obtained before fields or ruins can be harvested. (If you don't, your efforts could be construed as theft!) Gathering stone in quantity on federal land, such as a national forest or park, usually requires a permit. Inquire before gathering.

There's no shame in hiring someone to collect and cut stone for you. If the goal is to begin enjoying your stonescape as soon as possible, then conceiving a design and getting the wheels in motion to carry it out can bring sufficient satisfaction.

Surface granite at an abandoned quarry.

A road cut exposes dirt "lousy with stone."

River Rock for a Grill

I built a barbecue grill of stone for a friend at his lake house. The water in the lake was low and exposed a rocky shoal. We used a canoe to haul the stone, standing knee deep in the water to fill it. I was surprised that the canoe held about a quarter ton of stone each load. We walked the canoe full of stones over to his dock and hauled them up to his land. Five canoe loads supplied the project, all gathered on a Saturday afternoon.

chapter 3

TOOLS & MATERIALS

It takes just a few tools to become a mason: a trowel, a brick hammer, a level, a shovel, a hoe, and a wheelbarrow. Now that I've bought $40 thousand worth of tools and a pickup truck, I realize the short list of tools is still all it really takes. The other $39,800 worth of tools just makes the job easier, faster, and more accurate, which is what is expected of a professional.

At big building supply stores the masonry tool section is usually small because most store buyers don't have much field experience in masonry. Many tools in the carpentry section (where there are lots and lots of tools) can be used for masonry, however. Professional masons shop at stores that cater to their trade or order from catalogs or online. Good tools occasionally can be found at flea markets, and a few masons make their own.

Bigger is not always better. A 6-lb. sledgehammer may pack more punch with every blow, but it can wear you out much faster than a 2-lb. hammer, and the higher path is to pace yourself in hard work. Conversely, a hammer that is too light will glance off a chisel, have more missed swings, cause you to rare back too far (increasing fatigue and decreasing accuracy), and make too little progress. Like Goldilocks realized, the best tool is "just right."

For masonry, it is important to buy good tools. Cheap ones tear up so fast they are almost useless. As my tools wear out I replace them with the best and sturdiest tools I can find.

DIGGING TOOLS

• Mattock

A **mattock** has a thick oval hickory handle about 3 feet long. The flared end holds a loose-fitting ring with a scooping blade on one side of the ring and a hatchet-shaped blade on the other. It is used for breaking ground and loosening soil to be removed with a shovel. A mattock is a handy lever and fulcrum for prying stones from the ground and can trim neat corners in square ditches. It works well for both raring back or short light chopping strokes and is great for digging narrow trenches or dragging to mark lines in the dirt. Both ends will chop through roots, but the hatchet end works better. Keeping it sharp with a grinding wheel makes it more efficient.

• Posthole Digger

The **posthole digger** is the Ph.D. of digging tools for deep holes. Its two blades are curved and pointed and connected to two square hickory handles, rounded at the ends for an easy grip. The blades are inserted into the dirt with the handles held together, then spread apart, which grabs the dirt like closing fingers. You remove the dirt from the hole as you lift the tool. With a posthole digger, you can dig a hole 2 feet deep and 1 foot round in less than 15 minutes in most soil. It is used to dig deep footings for columns and for post legs in footings.

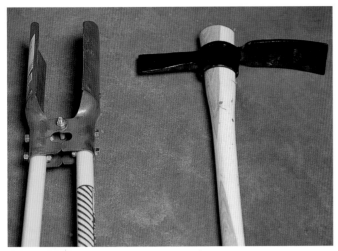

Left to right: Posthole digger, mattock.

Left to right: Spade, flat shovel, speed shovel, short-handled spade.

Hoes for mixing mortar, in two sizes.

• Spade

A **spade** is a rounded, pointed shovel. It will break ground in soft soil. Stepping on the folded lip at the top of the blade allows you to use your weight to sink the blade. A spade usually has a long rounded hickory handle that is narrower in the center. Fiberglass handles are more durable and allegedly absorb shock better but are impossible to repair if they break.

Flat Shovel

A **flat shovel** has a flat blade with square, tapered sides. It's used for shoveling out loose dirt, though it will break ground if the corner is used as a point. It will scale dirt smooth and holds more than a spade. It is preferred for shoveling sand for mortar mixing and scrapes a wheelbarrow cleaner. If I could take only one shovel to a job, it would be a flat shovel.

• Speed Shovel

A **speed shovel** has a narrow blade (2-5" wide) for digging trenches for water or drain pipes and electric and gas lines. It can be used in conjunction with a mattock for clearing loose dirt from trenches and can be used for breaking ground. Speed shovels come with long or short handles, but the long-handled versions are more popular.

• Short-Handled Shovels

Short-handled shovels are rarely used on masonry projects because they require more bending and put more strain on the lower back. They come with spade or flat ends and have open handles at the top.

• Hoes

Masonry **hoes** have two holes in their blades for aerating mortar and making pulling and pushing the hoe easier while mixing. They come in two basic sizes – the larger hoe is faster, but the smaller hoe is easier to work.

• Tampers

Tampers are used for compacting loose soil. A **hand tamper** is a flat, thick pad of steel with a hickory handle. You grab the handle at the top, lift the tool, and let it fall. A **power tamper** can be rented to tamp large paving areas to reduce settling. Building codes require structures to be located on undisturbed soil or on fill dirt that is tamped every 12".

MECHANIZED DIGGING EQUIPMENT

• The Ditchwitch

The **Ditchwitch** comes in many sizes, from slightly larger than a rototiller to tractor size. It has narrow scoop-shaped cutting blades extending on an arm that raises and lowers. It's used to dig narrow trenches for pipes and wires. It costs much less than a Bobcat to rent, and in a few minutes it will dig what an able-bodied person can dig in a day. Ask the rental store about half-day rates.

• Clay spade

A **clay spade** is a type of point for a jackhammer. Like a narrow shovel made of thick steel, it breaks up the hardest soil. It's available on request for electric jackhammers at tool rental stores.

• Bobcat

The **Bobcat** is the modern mule of masonry. It comes with buckets of various sizes and attachments that fit on its movable arms. It is small, can fit in tight spaces, and has a zero turning radius. It can be used to dig banks and footings, spread topsoil, and terrace. It can lift large stones and transfer over a half-ton of materials per load. Throttles for the wheels are operated by the hands with levers, and the bucket is operated by foot pedals. Although it's easy to rent one and operating skills can be developed quickly, hiring an owner/operator has its advantages.

TOOLS FOR BREAKING, CUTTING & SHAPING

• Brick Hammer

A **brick hammer or mason's hammer** has a square hammerhead on one end and a 1" wide chisel on the other. Wooden handles are most popular, but some brands offer metal or fiberglass handles with padded grips. Wooden and fiberglass handles are best for absorbing shock to the wrist and elbow, but one-piece metal-handled hammers are sturdier and can be used for prying and demolition.

The hammer's chisel end is used for trimming small and medium stones. The hammerhead is used for striking chisels, driving nails, and general hammering. Smaller, similarly shaped hammers called **tile hammers** can be useful for delicate trimming with the chisel end. **Never** strike a brick hammer with another hammer – a chip of tempered steel could become airborne.

Brick hammers of different sizes – the second one from the left has a fiberglass handle; the handles on the others are made of wood.

Sledgehammers.

• Claw Hammer

This typical carpenter's hammer comes with a straight or curved claw. The most popular **claw hammer** weighs 16 oz. It drives nails better than a mason's hammer and (unlike a mason's hammer) will pull nails. The steel used for claw hammers is more brittle than that of a mason's hammer and is inferior for striking chisels. A claw hammer is used for miscellaneous wood projects that arise on a masonry jobsite.

• Sledgehammers

Sledgehammers range from a short-handled 2-lb. hammer for striking chisels to a long-handled 12-lb. hammer used to break larger stones. I prefer a 2-3 lb. driving hammer, also called a "baby sledge," for shaping stone with a chisel. It allows me to get the same

Continued on next page

28

strike with just a wrist swing as I do raring back with a brick hammer. I never miss with a baby sledge. (Wish I could say the same about other hammers.)

• Stone Axes

Stone axes are used for breaking and rough-shaping stone. They are shaped like axes for splitting wood but are made of thicker, harder steel. The handles vary in length, increasing with the larger, heavier heads. A stone axe works better on stone lying on the ground than on stone on a cutting table, so using it takes more out of your back. The weight of the hammerhead determines the force of impact. Large stone axes have 60-lb. heads the size of mailboxes, and I have seen masons swing them one-handed (incredible!). Quick but brutish, stone axes are expensive. The smallest is about $40 and the largest over $100.

• Bushing Hammer

A **bushing hammer** looks like a meat tenderizing hammer but weighs a lot more. It is used to rough up smooth-sawn edges or to smooth and flatten rough-chiseled surfaces. It bludgeons away bits of stone.

• Deadblow Hammer

A **deadblow hammer** is shaped like a small sledgehammer, and its plastic-coated hammerhead is packed with metal beads that absorb the shock and bounce when you hit a stone. It's used to beat down flagstone into beds of granite dust or stiff mortar (If you're building walkways or patios, you need

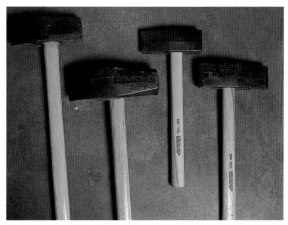
Stone axes of various sizes.

Carbide-tipped mason's chisels in various sizes. Chisels with carbide tips are the most durable and expensive. They are preferable for harder stone like granite.

one) and to beat on stones in a wall to tighten joints without making the stones bounce or breaking the bond of stones laid lower in the wall. I think of a deadblow hammer as a safe persuader, but if it hits a thumb it hurts worse than a metal-head hammer of the same weight. Most stone can't be cracked with a deadblow hammer even if you really wail on it. It's worthless for chiseling or cutting.

• Chisels

Masonry chisels are made with cold rolled steel. When a metal hammer strikes the softer steel of a masonry chisel, the top of the chisel will curl. The metal used in wood chisels is tempered, much more brittle, and may shatter. The most versatile chisel is 1" wide. Smaller chisels take off less, and so are safer, but slower.

Toothed chisels make "dotted" lines on the stone and go deeper with each stroke than a wide chisel. Unfortunately, they don't last long, and they can't be re-sharpened. A **point chisel** makes one deep "dot" at a time. It is very precise but slow.

A **stone set** is a chisel 4" wide. **Plugging chisels** are used mostly in repair work but when used for cutting stone, they sink deep with each stroke like a point. Designed to remove mortar joints, they are thin and flat at the point (as opposed to tapered) to fit between stone and brick without scarring the face of the material. When chiseling, the trick is to look at where the chisel meets the stone, not where you strike the chisel. It's a Zen thing – you learn with practice. Chisels with strike guards can block sight lines.

Tools for Breaking, Cutting & Shaping (cont.)

• Saws & Blades

Dry-cutting diamond saw blades range in size from 4" to 12 feet in diameter and are used for grinding and cutting all hard surfaces. I have two for my grinder – one is thicker for grinding out joints; the other is for cutting thin stones – and one for my 7-1/4" circular saw. I also have a wet saw with a movable table that takes a 14" blade (I use it mostly for brick) and a 12" miter saw. I buy dry-cut granite blades for all my saws, but I use water with them to cut down on the dust and drastically extend the life of the blade. Carborundum blades don't last long and are expensive for the few cuts they make.

Diamond blades are fairly expensive – 4" blades cost around $50; the 7-1/4" blade costs about $100; the 14" blade costs close to $400. The trick of making blades and saws last is to make multiple passes, each one a little deeper, instead of forcing the saw too deep in the material.

I use saws when shaping stone with chisels is impractical. The grit and dust from cutting stone with a saw will eventually tear

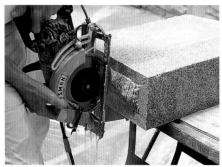

Saw modified with tubing for water.

up the saw – it's the cost of doing business. My Makita circular saw has endured 10 years of abuse cutting all sorts of hard surfaces and has only gone to the shop twice.

A **demolition saw** holds a 14" blade and is gas powered. Most are for dry cutting and when you rent one, the rental store checks the thickness of the blade with a micrometer or very precise caliper before and after rental and charges you for wear. Some rental stores have water-fed demolition saws (also called **bull saws**) with feeds that can be attached to a garden hose.

• Drills, Bits & Wedges

Another way to cut stone is to drill holes and use **splitting wedges**. Stone is drilled with a **hammer drill** that moves the drill bit up and down as it turns. Hammer drills are more expensive than drills that don't hammer and often don't have a variable speed feature. I have cordless drills that have a hammer setting but use them only when drilling small holes.

Masonry bits have flared tips and closer threads. Many have carbide tips for increased durability – they stay sharper longer.

MORTAR

• Mortar

Modern mortar is portland cement-based. **Portland cement** is made by heating a mixture of limestone and clay with oxides of calcium, aluminum, silicon, and iron in a kiln and pulverizing the resulting clinker, which is slightly adhesive but very inflexible.

When portland cement is mixed with **sand** and water, a chemical reaction creates a crystal that will harden into a substance that is similar to stone. (It's practically a geological event.) Sand also gives mortar volume and supports the weight of the stone. To provide flexibility, **lime** is added. Lime gives mortar body, loft, and plasticity that provides pliable, sculptural qualities necessary for jointing.

Cement is a generic name for mixes that are used to hold things together; mortar is a cement, but not all cement is mortar. Grout is the generic name for the material that fills the areas between stones in flat work (paving). **Concrete** contains gravel as well as sand and portland cement.

• Masonry Cement

Masonry cement is portland cement and lime in specific ratios noted by a grading system:

Type N Mortar (for general use) - 1 part portland, 1 part lime.
Type S Mortar (for high strength applications) - 1 part portland, 1/2 part lime.
Type O Mortar (for restoration of historic materials) - 1 part portland, 2 parts lime.

I don't use masonry cement except when I lay brick or block. The one advantage I can think of for using pre-mixed masonry cement for setting stone is that it comes in colors.

• Colored Mortar

A client wanted me to set dark gray river stone in orange red mortar for a small pond. His goal was to make the stone look like lava was oozing between the rocks. It was one of those special, speechless moments in the life of a mason that falls in the category of things-that-make-you-go-"mmmm."

Cement colors come in liquids or powders. Dry colors are added to mortar before adding water; liquid colors are added to the water used for the batch. My experience (despite manufacturer's claims) is that they fade every time. Most get a gray, washed-out appearance and go through several shades as the mortar cures over the course of a few years.

Safety Equipment

Appropriate safety equipment is essential for all masonry projects. First and foremost are **safety glasses**. One flying chip in the eye is enough to convince all but the most stubborn. Masonry dust scratches plastic and can obscure sight; cheap safety glasses can be disposed of without great loss. Wraparound sunglasses can substitute.

Ear protection is a must when operating saws, drills, and chipping hammers. Loud noises cause fatigue and headaches that decrease production, and hearing loss can't be replaced. Some tradespeople prefer plugs; I prefer muffs. In a pinch, cigarette filters will work.

Gloves are essential, and I wear pants with cargo pockets so I always have my gloves at hand. Heavy-duty cowhide driving gloves are the most versatile and durable. Always try on gloves before buying them. A glove that's too big will bunch up at the finger joints, making hands sore and causing a loss of dexterity. Gloves that are too tight constrict movement and accelerate fatigue. When chiseling, I wear a glove on my left hand (which holds the chisel) and keep my right hand bare to comfortably grip my hammer.

Kneepads are crucial when paving or building the lower portion of walls. Stone chips are unavoidable and one jabbed into the knee is not soon forgotten. Kneepads made for skaters are comfortable, and the hard plastic cover offers added protection against stone chips.

Dust masks and respirators should be used when dry-cut-

Clockwise from top left: Leather gloves, cloth gloves, ear plugs, goggles, cloth gloves with ribbed tops, ear muffs, rubber gloves.

ting stone with a saw and are recommended when working with dry cement and lime. Respirators that expel breath out the bottom of the mask will keep glasses from fogging. A damp handkerchief tied around the mouth and nose, while not a substitute, is better than nothing.

When sawing stone, wear safety glasses, ear protection, and a dust mask. Wearing a **hat** will protect your hair from grit.

Wheelbarrows, Handtrucks, Dollies & Wagons

A deep, heavy-duty **wheelbarrow** – preferably with a metal (not plastic) pan and inflatable tires – is required for masonry. (Smaller wheelbarrows with solid rubber tires and tubular steel handles are for gardening; inflatable tires allow the wheel to be manageable on rough terrain when loaded.) Wheelbarrows are used to transport stones and tools, for mixing mortar and concrete, and for transporting mortar mixed in another pan. Wheelbarrows with two tires are used mostly for pouring concrete. They are more stable and don't tip over as easily, but are less maneuverable and take more strength to lift and steer.

The most useful **handtruck** also has inflatable tires. If yours doesn't, put down paths of plywood or planks for use outdoors. I like the handtrucks used by landscapers to transport trees with root balls – they have large tires and wide carriages.

Dollies are low platforms with wheels. Stone can be loaded on them without much lifting. Dollies that consist of two wheels and a 1-ft. long, 6" wide piece of channel steel are used to move slabs.

Wagons with sides are fine for transporting smaller stones – the stones won't spill as the wagon rolls over bumpy terrain. Because they are usually low to the ground, less lifting is required.

TOOLS FOR LAYING STONE

• Trowels

More like my hand than any tool but my hand is my **trowel**. Trowels are used for shaping and spreading mortar, and the edge of a trowel can be used to trim small pieces of stone. Handle lengths and widths vary from one maker to the next, but a drop-forged one-piece steel is the only acceptable masonry trowel. Cheaper trowels with the blade welded to the handle shank are for other purposes (like spreading roofing tar) and are meant to be disposable.

Masonry trowels come in many shapes and sizes each for a different use. The most useful and common trowel for stonework is an 11" tapered version called a **brick trowel**. (I use a 10" to reduce the stress on my wrist, though it means I return to my mortar board more often.)

Margin trowels are square-shaped with blades about 1-1/2" wide and 4-5" long. They are used for shaping mortar and cutting straight lines in mortar beds. **Pointing trowels, caulking trowels, and tuck-pointers** are skinny trowels used to pack mortar between stones. They range in width from 3/16" to 1" and can be used to calibrate spacing between stones. I keep a 5" pointing trowel handy to carefully shape small amounts of mortar. **Flat trowels,** sometimes called "floats," are used to spread concrete and for plastering and stucco. Flat magnesium trowels are the most versatile when pouring footings and bring sand to the surface of concrete, yielding a finish like a typical sidewalk. Wooden trowels (usually mahogany) bring gravel to the surface for a rough pour. Steel trowels draw water or portland cream to the surface and are used to finish polished slabs.

Toothed trowels are used to set flagstone with thinset mortar made for tile setting.

Before buying a trowel, hold it and wave it around to check the balance, comfort, and feel. Narrow handles fit my hand better and rubber-clad "comfort trowels" are worth the extra expense. The blade should be somewhat flexible, but flexibility is a matter of preference. Trowels that are already broken in (with a worn, glossy patina to the handle) can be found at flea markets.

Left to right: 10" brick trowel, 5" pointing trowel, margin trowel, 1/4" tuck pointer, 3/8" tuck pointer, 5/8" tuck pointer.

Left to right: Finishing float trowel, magnesium float trowel, pool trowel, toothed trowel.

Tools for Laying Stone (cont.)

Be sure to clean your trowels after use (before lunch and at the end of the day) – if you don't, the accumulated mortar will alter the balance and affect the way mortar is spread and shaped.

• Pry Bars

Pry bars are chisel-shaped but are not necessarily chisels. They are 5-6 feet long and are used as levers to pry stone or lift cleaved slabs or are used in conjunction with posthole diggers to break up soil.

TOOLS FOR MEASURING & MARKING

• Measuring Tapes

A 25-ft., 1" wide **retractable metal tape** can be used to measure practically everything on a site. Most tradespeople have one clipped to their belt all day. In addition to a retractable tape, I keep a **folding rule** in my back pocket with one length unfolded for measuring less than a foot. Carpenters use a folding ruler with a slide extension on the first length, but the slide gets stuck from grit so this feature is impractical for masonry.

• Squares

Framing squares, which measure 16" by 24", are used to square up stones for corners. Right triangle **speed squares** are smaller (6" or 12") and less cumbersome, and they don't get bent and out of square like framing squares.

Adjustable squares, commonly called bevelers, are indispensable for repeated angle cuts like those that occur in angled walls. They are tightened with a wing nut and should be checked regularly to make sure they haven't slipped. The cheap ones last as long as the expensive ones, so there is no justification to buy one with a brass-trimmed rosewood handle if you're going to use it for masonry.

• Markers

Most stone can be marked with a metal point, such as a nail

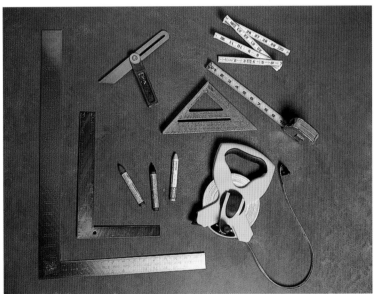

Clockwise from top right: Retractable metal tape, folding ruler, retractable cloth tape, markers, framing squares, adjustable square, speed square.

or the corner of a chisel, but I keep a **carpenter's pencil** in my pocket to mark lines. These pencils are flat and the soft graphite makes thick, dark lines. I usually snap a new pencil in half so it will take up less room in my pocket. I keep the pencil in the same pocket to reduce search time.

Water will wash away graphite marks, so if you're using a wet saw, mark with a **wax pencil** instead. Art supply stores carry colored wax pencils as do supply houses that cater to the granite countertop business – these are the best. Red, white, and black pencils can be used – choose a color that contrasts with the color of the stone.

Lead holders, once the standard for drafting, can be used to hold different color leads and eliminate the time needed for sharpening a pencil. Since most graphic artists now use computers instead of pencils, lead holders and colored leads are harder to find.

• Levels

The most useful levels are 4 feet or 2 feet long. Levels for masonry are made of wood. (Metal I-beam levels can get bent.) I prefer levels with yellow vials, as they are easier to see when wearing sunglasses. (Oldtimers call levels "whiskey sticks" because the vials are filled with alcohol.)

A **plumb bob**, a pointed metal weight with a string attached, is used to determine vertical string placement.

chapter 4

PREPARING A SITE

Preparing a jobsite properly saves time and makes a job easier. The more thought you put into it, the better it will be. Jim Hagen, a planner and designer, told me four rules for running a job:

Use good stuff.

Hire good folks.

Schedule everything.

Control cost.

Each rule can be broken down into countless sub-categories, but together they say it all. Good materials, good people, a plan. Don't unnecessarily compromise on something you will look at every day, or the whisper of regret ("I wish I hadn't cut corners") will last longer than the job. With stonework, a good job and a bad job are both hard work.

Planning and running a jobsite is a job in itself, even if you don't do any of the actual physical work. Like any skill, you learn it from someone who is good at it already or by trying it out yourself and making mistakes that you swear you won't repeat. A haphazard lunge – no matter how enthusiastic – is no substitute for calm, thorough analysis.

Start-to-Finish Planning

To plan a job from beginning to end, study the plans and look for anything that looks like it will be a problem and concentrate on it, running solutions through your head a few times from beginning to end. Do this with every phase and component of the project, and then figure out the order.

Finish-to-Start Planning

My technique is to figure the last thing I will do. Flip on the light switch for the step lighting? Okay, how does that relate to the first thing? Do I need to run conduit through the footing? Take power from the house panel box? Is a trash haul the last thing? Okay, will there be a pile small enough to haul with a pickup or do I need a Dumpster? Should the Dumpster be delivered before or after digging? I make a list of tasks and scan it repeatedly.

Starting at the end and working backwards as a planning technique has served me well. I have been told the Manhattan Project employed this technique to create the first atomic bomb. Though the results were dubious, the process was efficient.

Excavation

When you have planned and measured, it's time to start moving dirt. Practically everything built was, at one time, started by someone with a shovel. There's just no getting around it, I tell young laborers, and besides it's great exercise, takes true grit, and flattens the stomach. (A few mumble, "You don't dig much, do you?" Well, after 25 years of masonry, my joints are worn and the shock of impact hurts, but I have dug plenty and learned from guys who dig a lot.) Checking measurements as you dig is a natural way to step back and take a break.

Because damage to plants – and even occasionally pruning or cutting down trees – is often part of the building process, you may want to dig up and relocate perennials and shrubs as part of your preparation. If a tree is precious, drive in wooden stakes and build a barrier around it. The cost of the wood is nothing compared to the value of the tree.

If a project involves grading or more than a day's worth of digging, consider renting a Bobcat. No experience is required, and the driver who brings it will show you how to operate it. Bobcats move slowly, and in an hour or so you can get fairly handy with it. I've been told Elvis had one at Graceland – just for fun.

A Case Study In Excavation

My next door neighbor Jon Rembert was told by his wife that they needed a fence for their puppy. Jon said that before they put up a fence he wanted to grade and terrace the yard and build a stone wall and pond. He measured and drew plans. One Saturday evening, a Bobcat was delivered. Jon had never operated a Bobcat (he cuts hair for a living), but the driver who delivered the Bobcat showed Jon how to operate it, and Jon drove it off the trailer. The guys on the street moseyed over, most with beer in hand, to watch.

In the center of Jon's backyard was a pea gravel parking area. He wanted to plant the area in grass and use the gravel as a base for paving and as fill for his stone retaining wall, so he scraped up the gravel and piled it up in a corner. The area he planned to pave was grassy and had been used as a garden for years by the former owner, so Jon scraped up the rich dirt and stockpiled it. Then he spread the gravel in the area to be paved between his house and retaining wall.

Jon knew from measuring with a builder's level that he needed a compound slope that directed water away from his house toward the retaining wall with a second pitch that directed water toward the driveway. He used the Bobcat to cut the bank of dirt for his wall and created another pile of dirt from that. He spread the good garden soil for the grassy part of his yard and left a pile of gravel at the top of his yard to be brought to the retaining wall as needed, a wheelbarrow at a time.

By Sunday evening he had finished his grading. The Bobcat rental cost about $175. (An owner/operator would have charged him three or four times as much and taken half as much time but would not have let the neighbors take the Bobcat for a spin like Jon did.)

Jon spread grass seed over the center area of his yard and hooked up a sprinkler. In three days, the area looked like a chia pet. Planting grass seed immediately is a method of dirt storage – well-established grass stabilizes dirt and keeps it from becoming muddy runoff. The vehicle that delivers the stone will likely tear up the grass, and permanent planting will be addressed after cleanup at the end of the job.

Jon wrapped the borders of his yard with silt fence, a woven black fabric that keeps muddy water from running into the drainage system under the street. Silt fence was an appropriate precaution – one downpour can make a pretty big mess. Damage from construction runoff is truly an environmental crime. Aside from the unsightliness of muddy water, siltification of our streams and sewers suffocates fish, clogs drainage systems, and burdens water treatment facilities. Silt fence or bales of hay should be part of the package of supplies you acquire when breaking ground.

Staging

When excavation is finished, borders are secured to prevent runoff, and excess dirt is hauled away or piled up and covered with tarps, materials can be delivered and staged.

Stone Placement

Stone should be placed as close to the project as feasible. If it is delivered from a stoneyard on pallets with fence baskets, leave enough room to walk all around each pallet; don't put them right next to each other. The pallets should be at least 8 feet away from the wall. This distance allows you to spread the stone out flat near the work, which makes searching easier, and still have room (3-4 feet) to walk and kneel directly in front of the wall. I leave paths between groups of stones to make walking more surefooted.

Placing Sand & Mortar

Some thought should be put into sand and mortar placement as a mixing area will be a busy, messy place. I like to put sand on sheets of plywood. The smooth surface allows you to slide the shovel to the bottom of the pile without scraping any dirt. Dirt contaminates mortar with organic materials and mineral salts and can create voids. If possible, locate a mixing area near a water spigot. Look out for overhead wires and low branches if a large quantity of sand is to be delivered. Even a small dumptruck needs 20 feet of clearance to empty the bed. Cement should be stored off the ground on a makeshift or manufactured pallet and covered with two layers of plastic or tarps weighted down along the edges with stones.

Walkways for Working

I am a stickler about mud on a jobsite. I tighten my hoses with pliers, replace worn washers, even use two washers to make sure all my connections are drip free. Tripping on unsure footing can be a real disaster if you're carrying stone or pushing a wheelbarrow full of mortar. A twisted knee can put a person out of work for weeks.

I spread sand to help make walking less treacherous to and from the areas where I store tools and materials or mix mortar. If it gets muddy, I lay planks for the wheelbarrow. In front of walls, where I will be walking back and forth, I scrape the area smooth if it has ruts. During wet seasons, I lay down plywood to walk on.

Placing plywood in front of a wall makes the work area easier to clear of rubble underfoot – a flat shovel can scrape mortar and stone chips off a smooth surface easier than off the ground. I also use plywood to pile dirt for hand digging projects – it keeps loose dirt from messing up a lawn and can be shoveled up without scraping the grass away. I prefer 3/4" plywood, which doesn't curl like

Caged stone placed on a jobsite.

An area for mixing mortar is located away from the wall. A tarp covers the sand to protect it from rain, leaves and water.

thinner plywood. I cut the plywood sheet in half lengthwise, which makes two 2 foot x 8 foot pieces. They are lighter to carry and don't catch wind like a full sheet.

Precautions for Weather

During the fall, I rake leaves away from my work area to help keep tools from being lost. I keep sand covered to keep leaves and cats from contaminating my mortar. I never leave bags of cement uncovered overnight. I've taken to using tarps instead of roll plastic for this because they are more durable. Plastic sheeting won't withstand repeated rain and the sun's ultraviolet rays make it brittle. But I always keep a roll of plastic in my truckbox, in case of a sudden thunderstorm I can quickly cover my fresh work. If laid stone is flooded from a rain shower, joints will wash out, mortar will smear, a process called efflorescence will push white soluble salts down the face of a wall for years to come. This can be prevented by covering work if there is a threat of rain.

Temporary Access Roads

Clearing an access road and spreading gravel on it is an efficient way to provide supply and parking for a large job. It can save time and reduce the possibility of accidents and is relatively easy to undo when the job is complete. A temporary access road for a large job can make material delivery easier for sand, stone, and mortar or even a concrete truck, if poured footings or backing walls are to be used. It seems that everything in masonry is heavy, and if a big truck gets stuck in the mud, it is the homeowner, contractor, or whoever told the driver to drive there who gets stuck with the tow truck fee.

Avoiding Stains

To avoid stains on a driveway, cover the driveway with plastic or overlapping roofing paper and cover that with plywood. Plywood provides a durable surface for foot traffic, wheelbarrows, and mixing tools. If a mixing area is near a house or finished structure, roofing paper held up with duct tape or staples can shield against splashes and mortar stains on siding.

Jobsite Maintenance

When I run a job, I usually leave 20 minutes at the end of the day for cleanup. It's just part of good work – a clean jobsite is a safe jobsite.

Installing Infrastructure

Water lines, drainage pipes, and the electric supply should be installed before materials are delivered or concrete is poured. Whether plotted on a set of plans or figured on the

An electrical outlet supplied with wire through conduit.

site itself, provisions for infrastructure should be included when digging is being done. A Ditchwitch can be rented to help dig narrow passages for pipes and wires. (A Bobcat or front-in loader will remove too much dirt.) If trenching for utilities is not extensive, use a speed shovel. The narrow blade removes only the necessary amount of dirt. If the dirt is hard and compacted, break it up with a mattock first and clear the loose dirt with a speed shovel.

I use larger conduit and larger pipes as sheathing for utilities in poured footings. Placing conduit for wires and sheathing in smaller water pipes with larger pipes as tunnels is easy on the front end of a job. Later, if a pipe or wire fails, it can be removed from the tunnel by digging in front and behind a wall without destroying the wall. The pipes are easy to install during site preparation.

When I run wires or pipes underground, I put them at least 1 foot beneath the surface. My trenches are neat and about as wide as my foot. I walk in the trench to tamp the dirt before installing the utility. I place the wire or pipe in the trench and cover it with about 4" of dirt and tamp it by stomping. I run yellow caution tape on top of that dirt, then fill and tamp. If there is later digging, the caution tape will tell the digger to slow down and look.

Be sure to check with local regulations when doing electrical work. Contact your local government concerning proper permits and inspections.

Footings

Footings are the foundation your project rests on – they keep walls and columns from shifting into the ground. If mortar is to be used for stonework, the stonework must have a footing. The name "footing" is given to both the hole that you dig and the gravel or concrete that fills the hole, so explaining the process can get confusing.

A tidy ditch is recommended. Ideally, there should be no loose dirt in a footing – loose dirt will cause settling after the footing is loaded by the weight of a wall. There should be no roots or organic material of any kind protruding into the footing – they will cause voids in the concrete when they rot that will weaken the footing. I trim roots with pruning shears to remove them and slow their growth.

A footing should be free of water and mud. In clay soil, mud will cause the footing to slip and compress, infinitesimally diminishing the stability of a wall. Mud must be removed from footings before they are poured to pass inspection. One inspector told me that if the dirt in a footing would stick to his boot, I had to dig it out or let it dry before I poured.

To protect a footing from rain, an archeology student I hired one summer recommended that I line the footing with two layers of plastic sheeting as he had done on a dig. He pointed out that plastic was easily torn and that water pooling in the plastic would condense on the underside. I now follow this procedure if a footing is prepared and must be poured later. If it rains, water can be removed with a shop vac, a bailing bucket, or a small pump attached to a drill and garden hose.

Mixing Concrete for Footings

Concrete can be mixed by hand or with a power mixer, either gas or electric. Concrete also can be delivered "ready-mixed" by truck. Ready-mixed concrete is ordered by the cubic yard. A concrete truck holds nine yards (it's where the expression "the whole nine yards" comes from).

If I have a pour of more than half a yard, I use a mixer. If I have a pour of more than a yard, I call a truck. Ready-mix concrete is cheaper than the sand, gravel, portland, and the cost of the labor to mix it.

Small pours – for footings for columns or short walls – can be mixed either with loose materials or with bags of pre-mixed concrete. For pre-mixed, add water and mix. To make your own mix, use 1 part portland, 2 parts sand, and 3 parts gravel. A good batch for a wheelbarrow is 12 shovels gravel, 6 shovels sand, and 3 shovels portland. Dry-mix the materials first, and then add water. Too much water weakens the mix, but water is part of the portland crystal, so every grain should have water. Too little water makes concrete difficult to spread and settle and will result in voids and air pockets. Footings are best leveled with screed boards. It is worth the price of the lumber to drive in stakes and attach form boards.

A footing 8" thick is required by code in my area for most walls, but code requirements are the minimum, and exceeding minimum footing requirements delights inspectors. I never pour a footing less than 1 foot thick, and most footings I pour are 2 feet thick. For gateposts and columns, my footings are up to 3 feet thick. (Such overkill assures my columns never tilt.) In northern climates, the footing must be poured below the frost line because the ground's repeated freezing and heaving will move the footing if it's not deep enough. For guidance, consult your local building department.

A footing for a curved wall is dug and formed with Masonite and stakes. Parallel pieces of #3 rebar can be bent easily for the curve.

Mixed concrete is poured into the wheelbarrow.

If the ground is sloped, the footing may need to be stepped. Usually step-downs in footings are 8" to accommodate the height of block, but the footing should be level despite the slope of the ground. If the footing is stepped down, it must maintain a thickness of not less than 1 foot at the step down.

A stepped footing has been poured.

Leveling the footing

The curved footing, partially poured.

chapter 5

WORKING STONE

"All my days working with masons — oh, how they whine!
My knees, my wrist, my back."

Old laborer who helped me on a stone patio

STONE & THE BODY

Seeing a mother repeatedly pick up and put down a 60-lb. child is proof enough that stonework is an activity most physically capable people can do. The repetitive, deliberate motion of masonry can be rhythmic (like dancing) and make the body stronger. Eliminating unnecessary steps and unnecessary motion improves efficiency and saves time. If you can trim motion from your task, you will get more results with less effort and save strength. As with other physical activities, attention to movement calms stress and quiets the mind.

Stonework is harder than going to the gym, and each session lasts longer. As with any physical effort, attention should be paid to how your body reacts to strenuous activity. If you lead a fairly inactive life, getting in shape will reduce the stiffness and possible injuries associated with the lifting that stonework requires. Doing sit-ups will strengthen the back and stomach and tune the body's awareness to muscle contractions needed to lift. Tip: If you're building a stonescape around a hot tub, install the hot tub first. Cooling down too quickly causes stiffness (though the tendency after a day of sweating outdoors is to sit in air conditioning.)

Preventing Dehydration

Most symptoms associated with fatigue during physical activity, such as lack of concentration, muscle cramps, listlessness, and profuse sweating, are actually symptoms of dehydration. When sweating stops, that's the first warning sign of heatstroke. The nervous system uses water to transmit electrical impulses to the muscles and throughout the brain. In fact, brain tissue is composed of more water than any organ. For this reason, water is the best antidote to fatigue during exertion than any other drink. Sugar and caffeine further dehydrate the body, so colas and fruit juices – while refreshing – will not diminish soreness from physical activity. Alcohol also accelerates dehydration and can't replace what the body craves. Sports drinks often contain sugar and so should not be used as the only drink on a job.

Drinking water all day on a project is the best way to keep your muscles in shape as they adjust to strenuous activity. In the summer, my water bottle is never too far away, and some days I drink up to two gallons. Drinking that much water – and sweating – can deplete minerals, but eating mineral-rich foods (e.g., bananas, which supply potassium) and taking mineral supplements can compensate. Americans, I have read, have a higher tendency towards mineral deficiency than vitamin deficiency, and the results are most notable in muscle performance.

Dehydration is not exclusive to the hot weather of summer. Tradespeople suffer more back problems in winter, perhaps from the dehydration of drinking hot coffee all day, perhaps from caffeine. Caffeine causes muscle tissue to contract, so – to put it simply – you use more muscle for every task. A mason friend of mine was told by his doctor to decrease his coffee intake to two cups a day and drink two glasses of water for every cup of coffee and see if his back problem would clear up. He did, and it did.

Stretching

Stretching is another way to help your body with lifting before hard work but particularly afterward. A hot shower followed by a cool water rinse and moderate stretching increase blood flow to the muscles, "rinsing away" the chemicals that cause soreness.

Bending to build a low wall or set paving should be inter-

spersed with stretching. As my neighbor Jon learned when he built his low retaining wall, "It's all the up and down that gets you."

Elastic braces or bandages for the wrists, elbows, or knees – available at most drugstores – can help support joints stressed by repetitive motions and lifting. The best way to repair most minor injuries caused to joints and muscles is to rest. Pushing through the pain, a frequent mistake when working, can make a minor injury like a pulled shoulder take weeks to heal. Applying intelligence to the messages the body sends will help the body work another day.

Avoiding Injury

By listening to your body while you move, you can avoid excessive strain and injury and get used to doing heavy work in just a few sessions. Here are some tips:

When Lifting Stone:
- Keep the weight close to your body's center of gravity, not cantilevered away from your body.
- Squat low when lifting a stone, letting the muscles in the thighs do most of the work, not the muscles in the small of the back.
- Swing your butt out and low, using it as a counterweight as you get the weight of the stone nearer your center.

When Placing Stone:
- Get close to the wall when placing the stone to avoid the cantilever effect.
- Avoid twisting at the waist when setting down the stone.
- Adjust the position of your body so your toes face the wall.
- If you're setting a stone on the lower part of a wall, rest your elbows on your thighs.

Resting the elbow on the thigh when bending.

Sun Protection

Protecting yourself from the sun can't be overemphasized. Broad-brimmed hats are cumbersome when working around strings, but I usually wear a hat with a long bill, sometimes with a handkerchief in the back to protect my neck. I also keep a tube of sunscreen in my tool bag and slather up when I'm working.

MOVING STONE

Carrying Stone

Medium-sized stones can be comfortably carried under the arm like a large book. A firelog sack can carry several small stones in a way that won't spill them. A long loop of webbing can make a sling that gives an awkwardly-shaped stone a handle for carrying or for pulling up to a height with a rope.

Moving Heavy Stuff

A stagehand's motto says, "Never lift what you can drag, never drag what you can roll, never roll what you can leave."

On a jobsite, cranes and backhoes are rarely around when you need them. Only the simplest aids are available. If a stone is so heavy that two people can't handle it, find something with a wheel. A handtruck or wheelbarrow are the first choices. Let spotters guide and lend support to the lucky person who pushes the load.

Before a load is lifted, a walkthrough is required. Moving something should take twice as much time in preparation as in actually doing the moving. The path should be cleared of obstructions and swept. A team should appoint a leader (either

continued on next page

Moving Heavy Stuff (cont.)

the boss or the strongest person who has the most experience) who suggests a course of action, listens to other suggestions, and helps reach a consensus. (Only a foolish leader doesn't listen to others.) Let the leader call the heave-ho. Exhale on the push.

Ramps should be strong enough for the load but quick to assemble and take apart. I usually use two 2x10 planks and a piece of plywood cut in half lengthwise. I prop up the planks with brick and block, and use the plywood to make the transition from the plank to the ground smoother.

I have learned that a handtruck can move most big stones. Prying with crowbars for the initial lifting applies the fulcrum and lever that can move the world if they are long enough. Safety blocks (e.g., scraps of 2x4) can be slid under stone once they are lifted just a little to keep the stone from trapping your fingers if it gets away from you. Once a stone is set on edge, it can be pivoted on its corner and turned. Plywood scraps underneath the corner will help keep the stone from being damaged (and will tear up the plywood instead.)

Block and tackles, pulleys on beams held up with scaffold, come-a-longs, chain hoists, and all manner of mechanical-advantage devices can be employed, but what really lifts weight is the mind. Everyone involved with a lifting operation must stay focused. Any move should be announced before it is made. Concentrate and communicate. Turn off the radio. Allow yourself to recover after the weight is set – pant, drink water, complain, brag. Be very careful.

A plank and plywood ramp.

Moving a 500-lb. stone on a handtruck – one man pushing, two men guiding.

Using a handtruck to move a dimensioned stone.

Cutting Stone

The only way to learn to cut stone is to get an assortment of chisels and hammers and start beating away. Each stone is slightly different, and you must modify your approach with each cut. You will develop a workable cutting technique as you learn to "read" the stone, and you'll find some stone easier to cut than others. I have chiseled on many a stone for a half an hour before I got the shape I wanted. A few have fallen to pieces after getting the shape almost finished. This can be maddening, but try to exercise restraint. Stone comes in endless shapes, and there is always another stone to start carving.

Stone can be shaped to look like windblown fabric with just a few tools and a lot of time, but making stone look like something else is not the goal of this book. With the same tools, however, you can crack a stone along a straight line for a corner or a capstone at the top of the wall or take a little off an edge for a perfect fit.

Cutting stone will make you better at finding stone that doesn't need to be cut. There is, however, a sensation of being united with masons chiseling on stone throughout history that touches mythic feelings and makes working a stone into a shape rewarding in ways that are hard to articulate. I hope everyone who works stone can experience that. Stone has a tone and music that creeps through the tools and into the arms and hands as well as the ears and eyes. In time you, like thousands of ancient ancestors, will learn to read stone.

Choosing Stone for Cutting

Many of the problems about cutting stone can be eliminated in stone selection. Designing a project without straight corners is one way to avoid cutting, but working with stone is looking for stone. When I'm building a wall I measure the distance between two stones I laid with a folding ruler I keep in my back pocket, and then look for the stone that will fill the space. When I go to the stones that I've spread out on the ground I unfold the ruler enough to reach the ground, leaving the end flat out to the ground like a golf club. I look for the right shape and reach out and measure it. It keeps me from having to bend over so much as I search.

If there is a lot of cutting for a project, as with columns, look for stone that is not too dense or too layered with pores that are small and even. Compare its density and weight with other stones. I look for a stone that is the same color through and through. I ask myself if, when an edge is cut, it will be drastically different from the surface color. If cut edges of a weathered stone show, it makes a big difference in the overall look.

With quarried stone like limestone and granite, the face of the stone is not weathered so cutting into shapes is less noticeable.

Shaping Stone

To shape a stone, start by making a "dotted line" with a toothed chisel. Connect the chisel marks, and go deeper until it is time to flip the stone and repeat on the other side. The stone will eventually break (sometimes just where you want it to).

If cutting thick stone for a corner, allow enough extra stone to chisel and rough up the sawn surface to give it a pitched or "pillowed" shape.

Splitting Stone

1. Drill holes 6" apart in the stone.
2. Insert splitting wedges (they're made of two sheaths and a tapered pin) into the hole, placing the pin between the sheaths.
3. Drive the pin with a sledgehammer. The stone will eventually split along the lines of the holes. (You can hear it start to go; it's always thrilling to me.)

continued on next page

Granite slabs are hand chiseled for a dressed, pillowed edge.

Cutting Stone (cont.)

Boulders can be cleaved with wedges – quarries once used this process to separate huge slabs of stone from an outcrop, though now holes are bored with flames. Before power drills, a star-pointed chisel, turned a quarter turn with each hammer strike, was used to make holes for splitting.

Then, as now, removing dust from the hole increases the speed of drilling. Dust in a hole absorbs the shock of impact and dulls the drill bit. Hammer drills have a squeezable bulb with a tube to fit in the hole and blow the dust out. Blowing through a common drinking straw or plastic tube will also clear the hole, but be careful not to inhale the dust.

After splitting, drilled holes are often "dressed out" with a bushing hammer or chisels so the face of the stone looks chiseled.

Field Dressing

Most stone set today is field dressed (shaped on site) and trimmed with a brick hammer.

Here's How:

1. Hold a small stone in your hand. Scrape a line in the stone

Cutting stone on the edge of a table.

Chiseling a line.

Natural Shaping

There is an old story about a Japanese master gardener who found a stone on the beach. Near the center of the stone was a hole, about the size of a fist, that had been chiseled by the sea. The gardener, with great effort, struggled to move the stone, shifting its weight in the waves and clearing sand beneath it. The struggle with the stone took months of visits, until it faced the waves just as the gardener wanted. He would go to beach and watch his stone being carved by the sea, until finally he stopped his visits and by all appearances abandoned the endeavor. Years passed and the gardener grew old. He took his young apprentice to the stone and told him that now was the time to take the stone to his finest garden. The apprentice asked why he had not taken the stone to the garden before. The gardener replied simply, "It wasn't ready."

(this is called "scoring") with the corner of the chisel end of the brick hammer.

2. Score the line with the chisel end of the brick hammer until it breaks, gripping the stone tight in your palm or holding it with your fingertips (depending on how much shock you want with each strike).
   - Strike too hard, it will bust to pieces; too lightly, it won't do anything.
   - If the cut is stubborn, place the stone on the ground and beat on it. The stone will change pitch before it breaks – you can hear it.
3. *Option:* Flipping the stone and scoring it on all sides can give a more even break.

Table Cutting

Projects that have lots of corners and not much between them – like columns – require a more methodical approach for shaping and cutting the stone. If a lot of stone needs shaping, or the stones are big, a cutting table should be used. Larger stones take more time to shape, and kneeling to make each cut zaps your strength quickly.

My cutting table is built with 2x4s for legs. I have a piece of angle iron on one end of my table, and I built up the table top to just below the top edge of the angle iron. I use angle iron as a straight edge chisel for the underside of the stone. I can lay a stone on this steel edge and whack it with a hammer. It breaks along the steel edge – most of the time.

Memorial makers hand cut the most stone today. Their cutting tables are low, so the working surface of the stone is slightly below waist high. This allows for a lower drop of their swing and maximizes the hammer's effect. Chiseling on a table that is too high makes the shoulders rise more (which is tiring) and doesn't use the weight of the hammer efficiently.

Here's how people who chisel stone all day do it:

1. Draw a line with a wax pencil and a framing square.
2. About 1/2" from the wax line, chisel a line all the way across the stone. Use a wider chisel with a less tapered edge to spread impact on the established chiseled line. Angle the hammer and chisel away from the line. A few strokes with a 3-lb. hammer, and the excess stock falls away.
3. Back up the chisel to the wax line and, with a smaller hammer and chisel, follow the line. Some cutters hold down a square with suction cups and use the square as the guide for the final chiseling, taking off small pieces with each stroke. This is called "pitching the stone" because chips are flipped away from the stone as if they are thrown.

Tip: If you have tools on the table when you are beating on a stone, the tools will bounce around and fall off. Putting tools on another table keeps them at the proper height and makes them easier to find.

Cutting Fieldstone by Hand

Fieldstone is already weathered; when used in a wall, it has the look of old work even when it's new. If a rock needs shaping or trimming to provide a straight corner, flat base, or to fit closely between two adjacent stones already in place, the new (cut) face often is much lighter.

First, chisel as smooth a line as possible so a wider chisel and heavier hammer can spread the force of impact evenly. Natural stone such as fieldstone is never truly smooth – high points on the stone or chiseled line will catch a greater shock than lower points and can echo through the stone in unpredictable ways. Once a line is established and smoothed, use the chisel to remove large portions of stone.

When you chisel, lines of sedimentation in slates, schist, and limestone will direct impact to weaker areas of the stone and can de-laminate (separate) the layers. It may be possible to chisel-cut such stones a line a layer at a time. Stones that are prone to separate in sheets or layers can be trimmed against a piece of steel with just a hammerhead.

Chiseling vs. Sawing

On some jobs I can't avoid using a saw to cut stone, though I prefer a chiseled line. Chiseling is quieter, cleaner, and cheaper.

Marking a cut with a white wax pencil.

Marking a cut with a carpenter's pencil.

A hose laid on the stone floods the cut with water.

Stone may have pockets of dense ore that will overheat a blade and cause it to warp or break. (Flooding a cut with water will help prevent this.)

A dry saw can be modified into a wet saw with inexpensive plastic tubing and parts for automatic ice-maker lines and hooked directly to a garden hose. Manufactured water feeds can be bought at supply stores and from catalogs that cater to the granite countertop trade. They can be assembled and fitted on a common circular saw with just a few tools (like a drill and a screwdriver).

chapter 6

Placing & Mortaring Stone

It can make you really appreciate long stone walls to know that each stone was placed a few times before it was finally laid. How many times did hands touch the stone before the wall was finished? Placing stone takes time, but the goal of masonry is to be good, not fast. If something is built to last for centuries, it is foolish to hurry.

When using mortar in building walls, the stone should be "dry set" to test the fit *before* the mortar is spread. Dry setting shows you how much mortar you need to spread on top of the lower stone and confirms your stone selection. Laying the stone more than once in a space is just part of learning stonework. In time, fit can be predicted with more confidence, but nothing is as sure as test fitting. It also helps achieve smaller joints and decreases the need for trimming. Checking a fit between stones can be done with a tape, but checking the bed (the way a stone sits on the stone below it) is best.

Composition Basics

- "Laying one on two" is a phrase masons use to describe their craft in the simplest terms (e.g., "He lays one on two like no one's business"). Spanning two stones with one bonds stones together and reduces the number of vertical joints, which weaken a wall.
- "Tie through." Use "tie stones" to interlock the front layer of stone to the fill behind the wall.
- Many fieldstones are triangular. Their triangles can be used to create tight joints by laying the bases point to point and filling spaces at the back of the wall with rubble or by creating rows of points pointing up and rows of points pointing down to fill them.
- Placing wedge-shaped stone so most of the horizontal lines in a wall are slanted makes a wall less pleasing to the eye.
- Like I tell my help, "If it rocks, it ain't laid." Shims, chips, or mortar must be used to make natural stone stable as it sits.

- Lay flat stone level to the eye. Use a level, or back up and look.
- Leaning a short wall back at 1" a foot will hide imperfections.
- A retaining wall should *never* lean forward – it will topple in time.
- Make your joints less than three fingers wide.
- Don't use all the good stones first, or for fill.
- Distribute different stone sizes throughout the wall. *Note:* It is, however, best to place the largest stones at the bottom of a wall. They spread the weight of the wall over a larger area and provide a more stable base. Large stones at the base also get the work higher, faster and bring it up above your knees so you don't have to bend down so far.
- Break up horizontal lines with large stones that intrude into lower coursing.
- Don't top out a wall with all small stones.
- Stand up, back off, and look at your work from time to time.
- Stop working when you're tired. Pushing through exhaustion yields bad work.

MECHANICAL ASSISTANCE

In modern times, large boulders can be positioned by the forklift that delivers them to a home – usually for an hourly fee (in addition to the cost of the stone and the delivery.) Harnesses, chains, and cables are used to lower the boulders into prepared ditches and the boulders are stabilized with tamped soil, gravel, or cement. On well-funded jobs, a crane can be employed to place groupings of massive stones and boulders.

MORTARING BASICS

Mortar provides a matrix that unifies a wall, and most masons prefer stone to be laid with mortar. When it dries, mortar is the perfectly shaped shim. It is somewhat adhesive, cushions two stones one atop the other, and has a remarkable sculpting ability to adapt in shape and harden to a high compressive strength. Mortar is like stone in a liquid state. In nature, it's only found as lava.

Mortar is required if stone is used for cladding or veneer, to embed wall ties into a backing wall, or for keeping out water. If a wall is structural and holds up a building or is used for a bridge, it must be mortared.

Knowing the right mix for the application can determine the quality of the job. There is a lot of science to mortar – its ability to perform has been studied closely by engineers in the laboratory and masons working in the field.

Masons are often secretive about their mortar formulas, which they devise by trial and error and adapt to different applications by altering proportions and ingredients. They pride themselves on this alchemy. (One mason said to me, "My mixes are my business.") The basic recipe is 3 parts sand to 1 part portland.

Mortar should be formulated to match the hardness of the stone it will surround. The Egyptian mason in charge of the restoration of the Great Sphinx in 1998 was told to use portland cement to mortar the thin joints together as he replaced the eroded stones at the base of the Sphinx. He refused, saying the limestone was too soft to be set with portland. Like any mason who has repaired deteriorated mortar joints has observed, hard mortar will damage the face of soft stone as the stone weathers.

Mixing Mortar – Whoopin' Up a Batch

I mix mortar by hand, usually in a wheelbarrow. I roll the wheelbarrow near the sand pile and the pallet of cement sacks to concentrate the messiness of mixing in one small area, then roll the wheelbarrow to where I'm working.

Because I mostly work on old houses, I don't use a power mixer for mortar. Cleaning a mixer takes a lot of water, which makes a big mess when it is dumped after rinsing. Paddle

Mixes for Mortar

For setting most stone:
3 parts sand   1 part portland cement
Mix stiff with enough water so it holds its shape when squeezed into a ball but doesn't ooze between the fingers.

For walls, paving beds, tuckpointing joints, and grouting dimensioned limestone paving:
9 parts sand   2 parts portland cement
1 part lime
Mix stiff with enough water so it holds its shape when squeezed into a ball but doesn't ooze between the fingers.

For block and brick:
1 bag masonry cement (lime and portland are pre-mixed)
16 shovels of sand
Mix about as stiff as toothpaste, using about 3 gallons of water.

STUCCO RECIPE
8 parts sand   1 part portland cement
1-1/2 parts lime Mix like mortar. (See above.)

CONCRETE RECIPE
3 parts gravel   2 parts sand
1 part portland cement
Mix to combine. Add water. Concrete should be the consistency of mayonnaise.

mixers (used for mixing masonry cement to lay brick and block) make a mortar that is too fluffy to support the weight of stone, and they require more water for thorough blending than stone mortar should contain. Drum mixers used for concrete need gravel to blend the ingredients or too much water for laying stone, and they also require a lot of water for rinsing between batches.

Photo 1 - Dry ingredients in a wheelbarrow.

Photo 2 - Mixing the dry ingredients with a hoe.

Photo 3 - Mortar at the front of the wheelbarrow is too dry; in the middle, it's too wet. The mortar at the back is just right – it hold it shape when squeezed and released, but doesn't ooze through the fingers.

Wheelbarrow Batch

YOU'LL NEED:
9 shovels of sand
2 shovels portland cement
1 shovel lime
Water

Note: Water for mixing mortar should be free of salts, dirt, and organic material and should be cool. If your hose is laying in the sun, clear the hot water from the hose. If you don't, you will cause a flash set, which makes the mortar significantly weaker and more difficult to spread.

Heavy duty wheelbarrow, shovel, hoe, bucket for water (or a hose with a nozzle), gloves, and dust mask

HERE'S HOW:
1. Shovel the sand in the wheelbarrow, keeping a consistent amount in each shovel full.
2. Tear open the portland and lime sacks at the top so the tops of the bags can be rolled up to protect the unused portions from moisture and spillage. Using the same amount in each shovel full as you used for the sand, add the portland and lime to the wheelbarrow. *Caution:* If you have sinus problems or are sensitive to dust, be sure to wear a dust mask or a damp handkerchief. (photo 1)
3. Dry-mix the ingredients by pulling them toward you, moving to the opposite end of the wheelbarrow when the ingredients pile up. Repeat the process until the ingredients are mixed with no streaks. Be sure to drag the hoe to the bottom of the wheelbarrow where clumps of sand hide. Pick out any leaves or trash. (photo 2)
4. With the dry mix piled on one end of the wheelbarrow, add about a gallon of cool water to the empty end of the wheelbarrow.
5. Drag or chop sections of mortar (referred to as "sheets") about 1" or so thick off the dry mix with the hoe into the pool of water and pull and push the wet mix. Add small amounts of water as more dry mix is pulled in. Mortar for stonework should be fairly dry or it will ooze and drop down the face of the work as it is loaded with the weight of a stone. Ideally, it will hold together in a ball when squeezed with a fist but won't ooze out between your fingers. (photo 3)

Mixing gets easier with practice and is about the only aerobic exercise on a masonry job. Masons hire helpers to mix for them and to keep them supplied as they set and cut stone. (A skilled helper can mix a batch in less than five minutes.) Stopping to mix up a batch of mud makes a job go slower, but on an ongoing backyard project, mixing can help the lone mason pace the work day.

Mixing Tips & Cautions

- Be careful not to add too much water – a batch of mortar can be made unworkable with only a cup or two of excess water. If the mortar is too wet, it will tear and smear and drop on the face of the stone.
- Cover your sand. If sand is left uncovered, it may get wet and make measuring water more unpredictable. Sand will draw water from the edges of a pile through capillary action if it's not completely covered.
- If the mix is soupy, add sand first, then portland and lime to stiffen it up, pushing and pulling the mix until there are no streaks. Blending dry ingredients into wet mortar yields an inferior mix but will salvage a wet batch.
- Dry mixing mortar for later use is unfeasible because the slightest amount of water in the sand will start the curing process and will produce a mortar that is grainy, less workable, and very weak.
- Mixed mortar should be discarded when it is more than two hours old because it will start to set up (you can actually feel the heat), will form a poor bond, and will lose strength when spread.
- I don't use premixed bags of mortar. They are expensive except for the smallest jobs and yield a mix that feels gritty and is less workable. The sand used in premixed mortar is kiln-dried so the ingredients won't set up in the bag.

Tempering Mortar

In hot or dry conditions, mortar may need to have additional water added to improve its workability – this is called tempering. Adding water with a hose or directly from a bucket often will make the mortar too wet; pouring from an old (clean) soda bottle will help control the amount. Adding ice water will cool the mortar down and slow the setting time.

I add water to my mortar with a whitewash brush I leave in the water bucket near my mud board:

1. Make a depression in the center of the pile (like a volcano) and add the water there. Fold and drag the mortar into the water.

Tips for Working with Mortar

- To fully load a trowel, push the blade to the bottom of the board.
- To load a narrow strip of mortar (as when filling a narrow joint), flatten a place in the mortar with the back of the trowel and scoop up a small portion on the edge of the trowel.
- When bending over repeatedly to trowel mortar, rest the elbow of the hand not holding the trowel on your thigh instead of bracing your upper body with your wrist.
- Keeping mortar close by decreases the time it takes to get the mortar.
- If you're working low, put the mortar on a scrap of plywood on the ground instead of reaching up into a wheelbarrow.
- Decide if shovels full of mortar can be placed on a wall and then spread and shaped with a trowel instead of making a dozen trips back to the wheelbarrow.
- To shove mortar into a joint, push the mortar off the back of the trowel with a tuck pointer.

2. Shove your trowel into the mortar and slice back and forth to break up any chunks. (You can also mash the chunks on the mud board.)

Cleaning Up

- Always remove all old mortar from a wheelbarrow by scraping with a shovel and trowel or beating the wheelbarrow with a hammer. Rinse the wheelbarrow after each session or hardened lumps of old mortar will contaminate new mortar, causing stone set with it to rock and wobble as if there were gravel in the mix.
- Old mortar should be cleaned off tools with water. Have a bucket of water in the mixing area to dip shovels and hoes in.
- Mortar is dispensed more easily from a clean shovel, and a clean shovel weighs less.
- If mortar dries on tools, beat it off the tools with a hammer.
- When cleaning tools, it is tidier to make a small pile of dried mortar than to splash and rinse, as the dried mortar can be swept up.

chapter 7

STACKING & JOINTING STYLES

tacked stone can be drystacked or be jointed with mortar. **Drystacked** stone is stone stacked without mortar – the weight of the stone pressing downward holds it in place. The term may also refer to paving that is set in and/or surrounded by dirt, sand, granite dust, or gravel. **Mortared** joints can be hidden, raked, recessed, flush, or beaded.

JOINTING

In the same way music is made beautiful by the space between the notes, stonework is made beautiful by the space between the stones – the joints. Joints look best when they are consistent in width, depth, and texture. Here are descriptions of five basic types, from the least to the most visible:

- A **hidden mortar joint** mimics the look of drystacked stone because the mortar is placed so it can't be seen. For hidden mortar joints, mortar is spread on the back two-thirds of a stone, more than 1" away from the stone's face. If used on a stone veneer over block or a poured backing wall, hidden mortar joints require tight-fitting, regular stones to hold the wall ties.

- The mortar in a **recessed joint** is visible but set back – usually about 1" – from the face of the stone. Shadows created by recessed joints give a wall more depth.

River Rock - Drystacked

Irregular Flagstone - Drystacked

Guillotined Limestone - Jointed

Thick Veneer River Rock - Jointed

• In a **raked joint**, the mortar is depressed or slightly recessed so the edges of the stone are visible – the stones look bigger and the joints look smaller. Raked joints should be slightly lower than the edges of the stone and packed tightly.

• A **flush joint** is filled with mortar that is flush with the face of the stone.

• A **beaded joint** has additional mortar applied with a tool to create a raised, convex joint that makes the stone fit look incredibly even. The added mortar makes shadows that frame and define each stone.

Making Recessed Joints

HERE'S HOW:

1. A few minutes after you set a stone, fill in the joints until they are full and compressed. Wait until mortar is "thumbprint hard."
2. Come back and scrape away the mortar until the joint is recessed about 1". Use a tuckpointer or caulking trowel, which are designed to pack joints, or a stiff brush (like the kind used by auto mechanics to clean parts – an inexpensive one is fine). Scrape the brush clean every now and then to keep from smearing mortar on the stone.
3. Repack any joints that were loosened by this scraping.
4. Clean mortar smears and droppings before you leave the work at the end of each session.
   • Shoving towards the joint off the stone with a scrap of burlap the size of a washcloth or with an old glove can clean smears.
   • If a film remains after the smear dries, wipe it again. Dry burlap works best, but sometimes wetting a corner of a rag can help. Use a shop brush or finish brush to knock off mortar grit when it is good and dry at the end of the day.
   • A shop brush is best used diagonally to clean the stones – it won't put brush marks in the joints.
   • Step back and look for places you may have missed when you were close up. It really does make the job look a lot better.

> One afternoon, at the end of the day, I was fussing over joints in a wall. Tedious, tedious. I admitted to Bob Williams, a mason and stonecutter I've worked with for years, that I probably spend too much time on joint finish. Bob said in his clipped, understated way, "I don't think you can, not if you're any good."

Making Beaded Joints

Beaded joints, typically seen on granite walls and foundations of Craftsman-era houses, form a protective barrier against weather deterioration and saturation on the joints that hold the stone. They are shaped with a tool called a beader. For an authentic look, horizontal joints should cut through vertical joints.

A beaded joint should be applied to a flush joint that has set up for a day. To sculpt a beaded joint, use a very rich mortar mix: 2 parts sand, 1 part portland, 1/4 part lime. Mix beading mortar in small batches – a mix this rich will set up and be too hard to work in less than half an hour.

HERE'S HOW:

1. Mix the mortar.
2. Wet the joint. Take a ball of mortar in your hand. Press mortar on the set joint you finished the day before.
3. Dip the beader in water and rub it over the surface of the mortar you've pressed on the finished flush joint.
4. Flip off the scraps on the outside of the bead with a pointer, small trowel, or butter knife.

A wall with beaded joints.

Mortar Repairs

Mortar gets lighter in color as it ages. Once, when making a repair, I tried to match beige masonry cement; when I tore apart the old brickwork, I found that the original mortar was black. Only the outer 1/16th" exposed to weathering was beige.

Tooling a mortar joint so that it is scraped back from the face of the stone conceals the joint in shadow, which is one way to disguise that it is new work. Roughing up joint texture by punching the mortar with a stiff brush will add porosity to the surface of the mortar, and it will have an old look sooner.

New mortar doesn't look new after a few years. The upper portions of a wall will get dark first from saturation. Stains from molds and mosses will creep down to the lower joints eventually.

I make repairs with slightly darker mortar, knowing that it will get lighter. Setting stone in common mortar and scraping the joints deep so they can be tuckpointed later with colored mortar is another technique.

Right: A stone wall with beaded joints. Beaded joints are used on this cobblestone wall. The larger pointed stones, vertically placed, imply ramparts.

Below: A stone wall with plain joints. This fieldstone retaining wall has recessed mortar joints and a dimensioned granite coping.

chapter 8

SOLID STONE WALLS

Connecting to builders of the past by using the methods they used is a good history lesson, one that instills wisdom through understanding. Building a solid stone wall is such an undertaking.

Solid stone walls take up more space than veneered walls because their stability comes from their thickness. Typically, they are built as retaining walls. Sometimes a solid wall is a practical choice. In remote locations, such as beside a mountain stream, building a solid wall of local stone is easier and less expensive than trucking in storebought materials, especially if the stone is free.

Since only one side of a retaining wall is visible, using masonry fill or rubble is an economical way to provide the necessary thickness behind the stone face of the wall. Almost anything masonry will work. Scraps of concrete from a driveway set very well behind fieldstone and can be tied through by placing the fieldstone so it extends into the fill area. I know of one mason who visits a limestone fabricator almost weekly and rummages through his scraps and drops (the name given to trimmings from slabs) to use as backfill in garden walls.

Solid stone walls can be drystacked or mortared. A mortared wall needs weep holes or drains for managing water.

Dry Stacked Retaining Wall

This low stone wall is built of solid stone that was drystacked without mortar. The coping stones at the top of the wall and the stone steps were cemented for stability.

Right: Weep holes provide drainage in mortared stone walls.

A Drystacked Retaining Wall

Pictured on pages 52-53

Drystacked walls don't require poured footings. In fact, some masons just lay stone directly on dirt. For low walls, removing vegetation and scaling back the dirt a little is all that is necessary. A bed of gravel at least 2" thick is recommended as a base for a drystacked wall; gravel is self-compacting and gives a more stable base if contained in a dug shallow trench.

The downward force from the weight of the stone provides stability against wet earth pushing against it, which is why there is so much stone fill behind a drystacked retaining wall, to make it thicker and heavier.

Fig. 1 is a sectional drawing of a drystacked retaining wall 4 feet tall. For stability, it's deeper at its base than it is at the top. It's built in a shallow trench – the first course of stone is mostly underground and sits on a bed of gravel. The face of the wall is made of stones of various depths that extend into and mingle with the fill behind them. The fill includes gravel, which aids drainage.

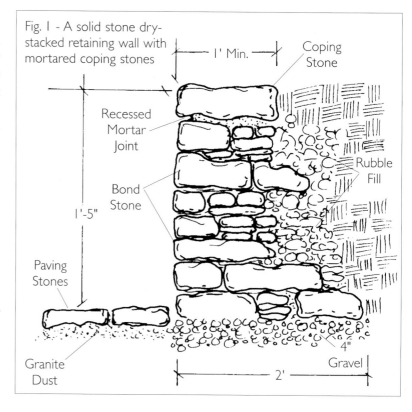

Fig. 1 - A solid stone dry-stacked retaining wall with mortared coping stones

1. Planning

Plan your wall. Lay out placement with a garden hose. Excavate or grade as needed. Clear away any dirt you dug from the area where you will be working by throwing it behind the wall or loading it in a wheelbarrow. Assemble your materials and tools.

2. Preparing the Footing

Remove loose dirt and rocks. Cut back any roots with pruning shears. Smooth the area where the wall will be built with a rake. *Options:* Tamp the dirt if it's not stable. Add a couple of inches of gravel.

3. Placing the First Stones

If you're planning to use guide strings and jigs, set them up. (They're not necessary for this low, slightly curved wall.) Lay large flat stones in the prepared space to follow the length and shape of the wall, placing gravel fill (gravel and dirt) in the spaces between the stones. If you're using a guide string, reference it as you work.

4. Adding Stones

Continue to add stones, using gravel fill in the spaces between the stones. The stones in the successive courses (layers) should be stable. Test the fit, making sure they don't rock from side to side or back to front. Use gravel fill to pack the spaces between the layers.

5. Mixing Mortar

The drystacking is complete. The coping stones, which will be set on mortar, are laid out. Enough space is left between the wall and the stones to walk and work. Now it's time to mix the mortar. Place dry ingredients and water in a wheelbarrow and mix with a hoe.

6. Placing the Coping Stones

Place the coping stones on top of the wall one at a time. Test the fit, remove the stone, add mortar to make a bed for the stone, and replace the stone. Do this for each one until all the coping stones are laid. Clean mortar from the tops of the stones as you work. Later, come back with more mortar and fill the joints, making the joints flush with the surface of the stone.

When we build, let us think that we build forever. Let it not be for present delight nor for present use alone. Let it be such work as our descendants will thank us for; and let us think, as we lay stone on stone, that a time is to come when those stones will be held sacred because our hands have touched them, and that men will say, as they look upon the labor and wrought substance of them, "See! This our father did for us." – John Ruskin

WALL WITH MORTARED JOINTS AND GRANITE CAPSTONE

This wall is an example of using two stone laying techniques. A portion of this wall is a solid wall of stone. This technique was used where the back of the wall would show. The section of the wall where the back would not show and that fit against a bank was built with the stone veneered to a block wall.

The wall is perpendicularly straight, with a beautiful curving flow as it outlines the patio. The straightness of the wall is achieved with the use of jigs as described on the following pages. The curve was composed around the dripline of Japanese maple.

Fig. 1 is a sectional view of a typical low retaining wall that might be built around a patio. Since it's topped with coping stones that are set in mortar for stability, the wall can be used for sitting or holding planters. The joints below the coping stones are recessed. The stone below the coping is drystacked, not mortared.

The stone below the coping is laid with a "hidden mortar joint." The mortar is scraped at least one inch from the face of the stone. Tight joints give the appearance of a drystacked wall.

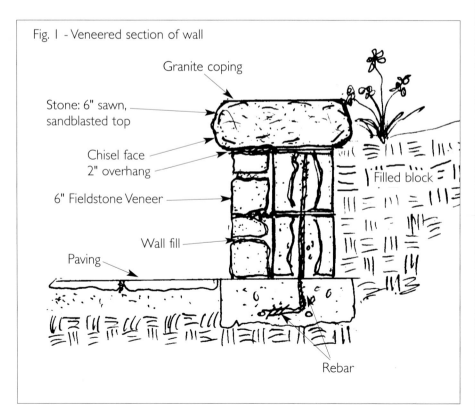

Fig. 1 - Veneered section of wall

Granite coping

Stone: 6" sawn, sandblasted top

Chisel face 2" overhang

6" Fieldstone Veneer

Wall fill

Paving

Filled block

Rebar

Building Jigs

Straight stone walls are first built with string. The string is the guide for the face of the wall (and the corners, if there are corners) throughout a project. Plumbing a string from an overhanging jig to a point on the ground or the footing where the wall will be built provides a reliable vertical guide for placing stone.

A tiny sliver of air must be maintained between the string and the stone, since stone, unless dimensioned (cut flat), is irregular in shape with high and low spots. Letting the stone touch the string will pull the string out of position, giving a false reading for the next stone. If a string gets out of level or plumb, it can't guide the rest of the wall.

Continued on next page

Fig. 2 - A flat wall with string jigs.

Notch

Notch

Nail with loop

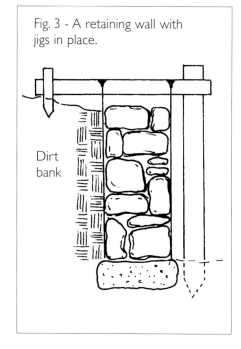

Fig. 3 - A retaining wall with jigs in place.

Dirt bank

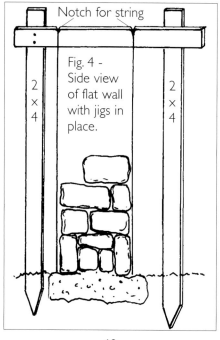

Notch for string

Fig. 4 - Side view of flat wall with jigs in place.

2 × 4

2 × 4

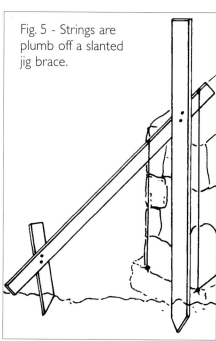

Fig. 5 - Strings are plumb off a slanted jig brace.

Building a jig – the wooden supports (2x4s or stakes or combinations of the two) that hold string in place – requires ingenuity because the string needs to be in place while you build but not be in the way. *Tip:* I often tie a loop on the end of my string and attach it to a nail on the back side of a stake. Carving a tiny notch on the corner of the stake where the string passes also gives a sure place to hook the string if you need to remove and replace it as you work.

Photo 1: Jig being constructed

Photo 2: Jig being constructed

Photo 3: A straight wall with jigs and string in place.

Photo 4: Closeup of jig in use.

Constructing the Wall

Photo 5: Footing was poured for this wall.

Photo 6: Leveling of footing.

Photo 7: Jigs and levels used as wall is constructed.

Photo 8: Patterns to be sent to fabricator were made for the cutting of the coping stones. Patterns were put in place to make sure they would fit.

Photo 9: Coping stones are placed. Wooden wedges used to shim and level the stones.

Photo 10: Checking level on coping stones.

This is a straight portion of the same wall pictured on pages 58 & 59 with mortared joints and a granite cap.

Walls with Hidden Mortar Joints

> *"I don't cut 'em, I find 'em."*
> Ray Hall, a fourth generation stone mason

Stones of various sizes and shapes were stacked and mortared to build this solid wall. The mortar in the joints was recessed 1". The seemingly random look is the result of careful planning and placement.

Solid Stone Wall with a Bluestone Cap

This solid stone wall has hidden mortar joints – the joints are so well hidden the wall appears to be drystacked. The bluestone coping is gauged (milled on two sides) to provide a level surface for seating and potted plants and has a dressed (chiseled) edge.

Solid Stone Wall Flanking Steps.

This solid stone retaining wall curves gently at the bottom of the steps. The stones of the wall rest on the granite slab steps.

chapter 9

VENEERED STONE WALLS

Because gathering, transporting, and placing stone that will never be seen is often impractical, most stone walls are actually stone veneer. High quality stone veneer is 6-8" thick.

A veneered wall frees up stylistic approaches for laying stone. Mortar must be used to set the stone, but applying mortar to the back two-thirds of the stone, creating hidden mortar joints, simulates drystacked solid stone with a lot less stone and labor. A backing wall also gives a mason something to build to, like a pattern or template, keeping the stone facing flatter with straighter lines at the top of the wall as well at the corners. Strings can be suspended from the backing wall and used to guide corners, and the top of the wall and be referenced for the finished height of the stonework.

Right: A veneer of quarried stone with hidden mortar joints covers a concrete block wall. The corbeled coping stones hang over the wall, creating a drip cap that helps protect the wall from moisture and a shadow on the wall that's an interesting design feature. Raising the capstone on the column emphasizes the corner, where walls of two heights meet.

Building a Veneered Stone Wall

In veneered walls, stone fill is replaced by formed and poured concrete or reinforced cinderblock, where the cavities in the block are filled with cement and vertical steel rods known as rebar that are imbedded in the footings. Stone is set in front of the backing wall and joined to it with metal ties. The ties are attached to the backing wall and laid in the mortar joints between the stones, and the cavities behind the stone are filled with mortar. Using a reinforced wall as a backing reduces the need for the substantial thickness at the base of the wall and allows the stone to be used only on the parts that show, like cladding. This method is the process most contractors use.

Block work goes up fast and is cheap compared to all other types of masonry, both in labor and materials. A reasonable approach to building a series of retaining walls for a backyard renovation is to have a mason pour footings and lay up the block and have the homeowner veneer them with stone. All the good parts of laying stone – cutting, finding, fitting – can still be learned and enjoyed.

Level blockwork can be used as a guide to keep veneered stones level – simply compare lines of the stonework to the joints of the block. If a wall has a sloping shape at the top, block can be cut lengthwise with a saw to help guide the dimensions of the wall.

Stainless steel wall ties connect the block wall to the stone veneer. Wall ties are easily bent but prevent lateral movement of the stone.

Working with Block

Modern cinderblocks are made from slag, which is a by-product of burning coal, and most blocks have two holes called cells. The web at the center of the block is used like a handle for lifting and placing. Most block orders include "halfs" that are molded to be half a block wide.

Because blocks are square and modular, they bond in perfect patterns of one on two and are easy to adjust on a stiff, fluffy mortar. They cut easily with a brick hammer, chisel, or saw. To cut a block with a brick hammer make a dotted line with the corner of the chisel end, flip the block, and repeat on the other side. The block will change pitch right before it breaks.

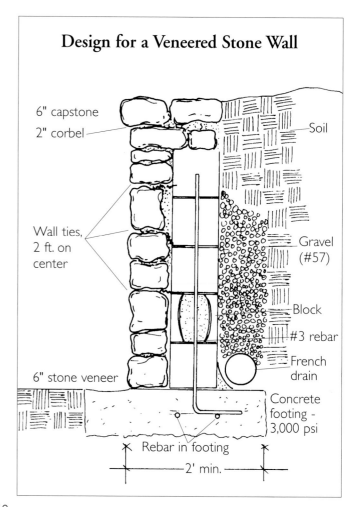

Design for a Veneered Stone Wall

6" capstone
2" corbel
Soil
Wall ties, 2 ft. on center
Gravel (#57)
Block
#3 rebar
French drain
6" stone veneer
Concrete footing - 3,000 psi
Rebar in footing
2' min.

Photo 1 - The first course.

Getting Started

Plan your wall, including drainage. Lay out placement with a garden hose or strings, stakes and lumber. Measure. Excavate or grade as needed. Assemble your materials and tools. Dig and pour footings. Build and install jigs. Mix mortar in a wheelbarrow with a hoe.

Laying a Block Wall

1. Lay the first course on the footing. (photo 1) If the footing is level, long spans of block work can be leveled by measuring from the footing or checked with a line level. Set the corner blocks first.

   • To spread mortar on a block (called "buttering" in the trade) stand the block on end and scrape mortar off the trowel on the end of the block. The motion should be swift. To butter the bed (horizontal) joint of the block, scrape mortar off the trowel with the edge of the block that has been laid.

   • More mortar is used on the first course or layer as it is spread on the footing for the full 8" width of the block.

   • The most certain way to space blocks properly is to set the first course in place without mortar, leaving 1/2" between each block. Mark the end of each on the footing. Remove the blocks. Follow the marks when you begin the wall.

Continued on next page

Photo 2 - A wall tie embedded in mortar.

Photo 3 - A block being buttered with mortar.

Photo 3 - Adding the second course of block. Note the string used as a guide for leveling. (You can't see the wall ties – they're on the other side of the wall.)

Laying a Block Wall (cont.)

2. Embed wall ties in the mortar about 2 feet apart on center. (photo 2)

3. Add the second course of block. (photo 4) Make sure each block is level and plumb; adjust by moving and tilting it on the mortar. Scrape away excess mortar with a trowel as you adjust. (photo 5)

4. Continue adding block until the wall is the desired height. The joints don't need to be particularly neat – they're going to be covered up, remember – just be sure the blocks are level and plumb. (photo 6)

Photo 5 - Excess mortar is scraped away with a trowel as the block is adjusted.

Photo 6 - A block wall with wall ties in place. On this part of the wall, brick were used as a first course to accommodate the intended height of the finished wall.

Photo 7 - The stone veneer is nearly complete. The backing wall provides a place other than the ground to distribute materials. If small stone are used for the facing, the stone can be set on top of the backing wall and selected for placement, reducing the need to stoop.

Photo 8 - A corner of the wall. For emphasis, the stone on the wall is deeper at the corner.

Applying the Stone Veneer

When the mortar on the block wall is dry, you're ready to start applying the stone veneer. Stage the materials. Build jigs and attach strings. Decide how the finished joints are going to look (hidden, recessed, raked, or flush). Mix the mortar.

1. Start laying stone at the base of the wall, placing it in front of the block on the footing, using your strings as a guide. For a wall with a plumb face, the stones should be the same depth (or close to it). Fill the cavities behind the stone with mortar.
2. Build the corners of the wall. Check your guide strings and make sure the jig hasn't shifted. Lay the wall ties in the mortar joints between the stones to "tie" the stone to the backing wall.
3. Fill in between the corners with stone, laying one on two and tying through, filling the cavities between the block and the stone with mortar. Follow and check your strings. Keep adding stone until the top of the veneer is level with the top of the backing wall.
4. Test fit and mortar underneath the flat stones at the top of the wall, working one stone at a time.
5. Add mortar to the joints between the stones, making the joints flush for a smooth top.

A portion of the finished wall. The block is completely covered with stone. The hidden mortar joints give the look of a drys-tacked wall. The wall is capped with thick stones trimmed and set with flush joints to form a slightly irregular but basically straight and flat top.

This is a veneered retaining wall along a sidewalk. The stone is fieldstone with recessed mortared joints and has a cap of slate. The attractive planting beds are at eye level.

This fieldstone retaining wall is nearly 5 feet tall at one end. The mortar is recessed with fieldstone coping.

Left: This section is the same stone wall as shown at left. The stone wall is lower at one end. Instead of stepping the wall down it is simply sloped. The coping stone helps this transition and makes a finished look. The sloping rather than the stepping reduces price and materials.

Below: On this stone wall, a long stone was cantilevered for interest. It makes a wonderful place to hang a hose or sit a pot.

Left: This section is the same wall as at right, showing the area of the steps. The steps and walk are created from the same dimensioned flagstone as the capstones.

Right: This low retaining wall is made of flagstone with dimensioned capstones. Using flagstone is great for a do-it-yourself project because it is lighter and thinner, making it easier to handle.

Right: This is an old stone retaining wall made of random irregular stones with recessed mortar. Stones are made more beautiful with age as the moss and the weather gives the stones character.

Right: This veneered retaining wall borders a lovely flag-stone path. The retaining wall has recessed mortar joints in a pattern of one over two. Moss and lichen add beauty to this old wall.

Below: The pattern of one over two on this curved retaining wall add strong horizontal lines to the wall.

chapter 10

COLUMNS OF STONE

Columns are short walls built for different purposes – sometimes as a focal point at the end of a wall, usually to attach a gate to join a wooden or metal fence. It is always a problem attaching another structure to stone. Attaching to a column means relying on the stone or joint to support the cantilevered weight of the gate or fence.

Engineered attaching devices for masonry are invented almost every day and include shields, hardened screws, and epoxy fillers. They all require pre-drilling with hammer drills and masonry bits. (Luckily, these tools can be rented.) Most fasteners fail eventually. Movement and swelling wallows out the hold. Constant stress on the stone may crack it.

To make the gates last, gate installers prefer to hang their gates on a steel post with welded arms called "look-outs" attached to the steel core. (They are called look-outs because they stick out and catch the shins or bump the heads of people working around them. For safety, I cover look-outs with an old glove stuffed with paper to soften the inevitable blows and am delighted when they are finally surrounded with stone.) When the gate is installed, the gate's hinges are welded to the look-outs. The look-outs and all metal in stonework should be primed with a rust-inhibiting metal primer before installation to deter rusting, which will expand the metal and crack the stone apart eventually.

HOW TO BUILD A COLUMN

Columns lean because of inadequate footings – usually the footings aren't deep enough. A small point load in the soil, which a 2-ft. foot wide column makes, will shift. Digging a deep footing stabilizes the concrete by friction against the sides of the dirt.

1. For a stable column, dig and pour a footing no less than 2 feet deep and 4" wider than the outside dimensions of the column. If built for a gate, install a 4" x 4" thick-walled steel post as the footing is poured. Hold the steel post plumb in place with angled 2x4 braces that are clamped securely to the column and staked securely in the dirt. (Fig. 1)

2. Once the footing is poured, double-check the steel post for plumb and alignment – it may twist.

3. When the footing is cured around the steel post, attach a plywood form to the top of the post the size of the base of the column.

4. Draw the locations of the corners of the column on the footing and locate strings with a plumb bob to the plywood guide at the top of the steel column.

5. Weld look-outs for the hinges (flat steel 1/2" thick, welded to the post or screwed on with self-tapping metal screws) so they extend 1-1/2" beyond the face of the upcoming stonework. (Fig. 2)

6. Lay stone, interlocking corners and tying through to the post with tie stones.

Continued on next page

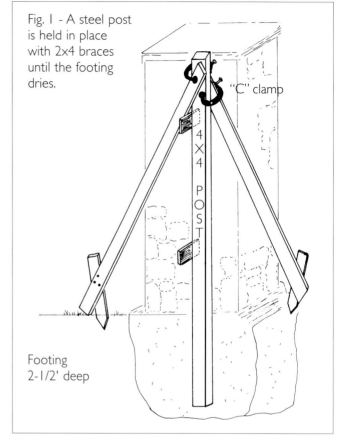

Fig. 1 - A steel post is held in place with 2x4 braces until the footing dries.

"C" clamp

4 X 4 POST

Footing 2-1/2' deep

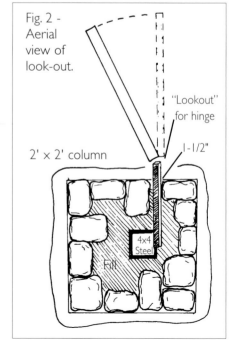

Fig. 2 - Aerial view of look-out.

"Lookout" for hinge

1-1/2"

2' x 2' column

4x4 Steel

Fill

Columns for a Fence

If columns are built for a wooden fence, it is easier to put wooden 4x4s in the footing spaced the width of the column and attach the fence to them. The wooden 4x4s can be used as guides to reference the shape and plumb of the stone column or to hold a jig for string guides. (Figs. 3 and 4)

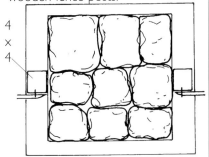

Fig. 3 - Aerial view of column with wooden fence posts.

4
x
4

Fig. 4 - Elevation of column with wooden fence posts.

Using Scaffolding

If a column is over 6 feet high, I set up scaffolding to set the top stones. Ladders are for other trades – they can't take the weight of masonry. Masons use scaffolding. It doesn't take but a few minutes to set up scaffolding, and it is the safest way to work on something high. Good scaffolding lets you concentrate on the work and not your feet.

Scaffolding can be rented – it's not something you have to buy. The purpose of scaffolding is to serve the body in its work. If you have to bend way over when working on scaffolding, you set it up wrong. Scaffolding should be easy to set up and strong enough to support the weight and movement of work, and it should come apart easily. Bases for walkboards should be stable, and walking surfaces should be kept clear of stone chips and obstructions. Wobbly walkboards make working more difficult.

If you have to elevate to set stone, you also must raise materials. Scaffolding has rungs so walkboards can be placed below material boards to put supplies at waist height.

Column-Building Tips

- For short columns, cornerstones can be plumbed with a 4-ft. level (but a level is never as sure as strings).

- Measure the column to make sure it doesn't get wider as it gets higher.

- Cornerstones chiseled and checked with a square are advised for columns.

- A concrete block core veneered with stone is easier to build than a solid stone column, but it may not be suitable for a purist.

chapter 11

PATHS & WALKWAYS

Paths, stepping stones, and walkways provide paved areas for feet and let people know where you want them to walk. All are easy projects for beginners.

STEPPING STONES

Stepping stones are placed so the feet will land on them in the natural rhythm of walking. Flat stones 1" or so thick are spaced so that with each step the walker's foot lands on a stone, not the surrounding dirt, gravel, or grass. They should not wobble or rock.

To set stepping stones:
1. Clear the area underneath where you want to place them of plant material and rocks. Use the stone as a pattern – place it and, with a small trowel, mark the outline of the stone.
2. Depending on the depth of the stone and whether you want them to be flush with the ground or raised, you may want to dig holes to hold them.

3. Smooth the area under the stone by adding sand or pea gravel.
4. Put the stones in place, tapping or twisting for a secure fit.

Stepping stones that lead up a hill can be placed securely by carefully digging a pocket to hold them. An inch or two of gravel provides a stable base for infrequently used stepping stones; a shovel or two of cement underneath them will make them even more stable and is a good idea if, for example, the stepping stones lead to a birdbath that may need filling every few days.

Right: In this Asian-inspired garden, a path of thick (about 4") stepping stones leads to a koi pond. A carved stone lantern extends the theme. These stones are interplanted with mondo grass; any low-growing groundcover could be used.

A SIMPLE STONE PATH

If conditions are right, nothing is simpler in all of masonry than a stone path. Preparation may involve only raking.

HERE'S HOW:

1. Dig away the grass (or weeds or other plant material), removing the roots and clinging soil. Tip: Put the grass in a bucket to carry off or place the dirt and grass on a scrap of plywood to make it easier to shovel into a wheelbarrow later.
2. Sprinkle a substrate – sand, granite dust, or dry pack (3 parts sand and 1 part portland cement) – where you dug.
3. Place the stone and tamp down by tapping it with a hammer handle or a dead-blow hammer or by striking a scrap of wood with a hammer until the stone is at the desired height and is stable. (Remember, if it rocks, it ain't laid.)
4. Repeat this procedure until you have reached your destination.

CONSIDERATIONS

• Make sure the setting bed is full by listening to the stone as you beat it into place. Hollow sounds are voids, and the unsupported part of the stone may crack when stepped on if there are voids.
• Lifting the stone after you have seated it in the substrate and inspecting the bed for voids is advised. Most stones are laid more than once to be sure they are seated thoroughly.
• Larger stones require more preparation.
• Thicker stones mean deeper digging, but they are more stable.
• On a hill, stone 6" thick may help provide a better path.
• Slanted paving stones are unstable, and the substrate (sand or granite dust) will likely wash out (especially if the path receives a large volume of running water during a downpour).

Minimal preparation is required when thick paving stones are used.

Placing stone in a gravel path creates a permeable surface that allows water to flow through. One course of fieldstone is used along the sides of the path as a border.

WALKWAYS

A walkway is more durable than stepping stones or a path and is used in areas that receive more traffic. The stones are fitted together more carefully and may require trimming with a hammer, a chisel, or even a masonry blade on a circular saw.

Preparation for a walkway involves digging away the grass and removing any stones or dirt clods that may make the stone rock when it is laid. For a curving walkway, lay out the shape with a garden hose and spray with marker paint prior to scaling back the dirt.

Above: For those who believe "moss is boss," only a dry-laid walk will do. The stone is placed in dirt. In shady areas, moss will grow up and around the stone.

Setting a Walkway in Sand

If you choose to set the stone in sand, lining the excavated walkway with thick plastic (6 mil) or roofing paper will keep the sand from washing into the dirt. Avoid joints over three fingers wide – rain washes away sand in wide joints. Granite dust makes a sturdier base than sand and packs down tighter.

1. Set a stone in the sand or granite dust and tap it down to the right height.
2. Tap sand in the joint around the stone so that it packs tightly around the edges.

Options for Walkways with Sand:
• Sweep sand into the joints. Spray lightly with a hose repeatedly until the sand settles flush to the stone.
• Sweep in potting soil and seed with grass seed.
• Sweep in potting soil and add seeds of aromatic plants like English thyme, mint, or chamomile to create a fragrant walk as the plants are brushed by foot traffic.
• In shady spots, mosses will grow in the joints adding vibrant contrasts in color to slates and flagstones.

Grouted Walkways

If the walkway receives a lot of running water, washout can be a problem – granite dust and sand will wash away before plants can stabilize the joints. And if a walkway receives heavy traffic, jointing the stone with mortar is the best way to keep the stones in place. There are almost as many methods to grouting paved stone as there are masons.

Regardless of the grouting method, the cement bed should be cleaned of loose dust, sand, and debris. A whisk broom is typically used, but a shop-type vacuum cleaner clears the joints even better.

Wet Grouting Methods

One mason I know uses a very soupy mix of sand and portland cement (3:1), pouring it into the joints with a beer pitcher. He then uses a small trowel to cut the joint flush to the stone. Another I know uses a gravy ladle. Still others use a grout bag (like the pastry bag bakers use for decorating cakes, but made of heavy vinyl for masons) and come back and cut the joints flush to the stone with a small trowel.

Some masons mix soupy mortar and pour the mortar all over the walkway, then drag soaked burlap sacks over the stone to push the mortar into the joints. They rinse the sacks in buckets of water, dragging over and over until the joints are full and there is only a slight film of mortar staining the stone. The next day, they scrub lightly with a muriatic acid solution (10 parts water to 1 part muriatic acid) to wash away the remaining mortar – hopefully.

Disadvantages to Wet Grouting

A wet joint is a weaker joint. It will wear away and pit with exposure to the elements. The compression ratio is much lower, and it is prone to shrinking and cracking as it cures. Sometimes voids or bubbles form that eventually crack and fail. It is fast, though.

Many stones (notably limestone, marble, and slate) discolor if muriatic acid is applied for cleaning, and mortar smears will age differently than the stone does.

Wet grouting is messy. A kicked-over bucket of soupy grout is a calamity that must be cleaned up immediately, so you need to keep water, sponges, and rags on hand to wipe up the mess. Loading a grout bag or pitcher splatters mortar, though keeping the bucket on a scrap of plywood minimizes the mess of drips and spillage.

Using a grout bag requires wrist strength and may lead to minor sprains.

This slate path along the side of a house has black mortared joints and is bordered by salvaged bricks.

Dry Pack Grouting

I don't use wet grouting methods. My favorite method is to dry pack joints the day after the stone is laid.

I keep the dry pack (3 parts sand, 1 part portland cement) mix in a bucket beside me and dip it out with a trowel. I load it in the joint, compress it with a pointing trowel until it fills the joint, and cut off the excess with a small trowel until the joint is flush to the stones.

With really large stones or for a patio that receives a lot of water runoff, I carefully paint the joint with portland neat (water and portland cement the thickness of paint) before packing the joint. I use a small paint brush. (Be sure to keep a damp sponge and water handy for rinsing away any drops that spill from the moving brush.)

Left: This borderless walkway has mortared joints. To achieve the clean edges, mortar is cut away from the stone before it dries completely.

Above: For a walkway that gets frequent use, it's best to set paving stones in cement.

Right: Stones cut from an architect's pattern are placed on formed and poured cement pads. The stones have mortared joints.

chapter 12

PATIOS

Patios make great outdoor rooms for dining, for entertaining, and for quiet contemplation. Furniture can be placed on them, and low walls with dimensioned coping can be built around them, creating natural spots for gathering and relaxing.

Stone paving set in cement and grouted with cement becomes an impermeable surface. Paving set in sand or granite dust will let a lot of surface water be absorbed into the soil. A patio can be the most outstanding built feature of a garden. If sloped properly, it can serve as a drainage solution for a yard that slants towards a house.

When you build a patio, there's no way around it – you're going to be spending some time on your knees. Don't wait until it hurts – use kneepads!

Right: A sloped patio can be a drainage solution, directing water the way you want it to flow. This flagstone patio has irregular-shaped stones and mortared joints of similar size – the regularity of the joints keeps the look from getting too haphazard. The patio is bordered by a low, curved fieldstone wall. The coping and steps are made of sandblasted chisel-faced granite.

PATIO DESIGN

Managing a high volume of water on a patio is the most important consideration of the design, and every design is different. If a patio is large, drain boxes and grates can be installed and the patio can be divided into sections, with each section sloping to the drain boxes. Installing and connecting the drain boxes makes a project more technical; if the drains lead to a central collection pipe, you may wish to consult a civil engineer or drainage specialist for advice.

When laying a patio, take great pains to get the perimeter of the patio true to the string so the slope will be correct. Then wrap string around bricks and lay them on your perimeter stones, stretching the string tightly. If you have a compound slope, use strings coming from both slopes to check the level.

PLANNING FOR DRAINAGE

Sending the water away from the house and into the yard is often all that's necessary to solve a drainage problem; depending on where the water will exit the yard, a compound slope (such as away from the house and off to one side) may be required to completely deal with the water.

If the patio slopes away from the house and towards a retaining wall, the wall may act as the guide (like the bottom of a creek bed), directing the water off to one side. Or a patio can be crowned (have its high point) in the center and the water can slope away from the house and to a far corner, then course down the side yard of the house.

Whatever method of managing runoff you choose, think about it real hard. The best rule of thumb is to slope flatwork (as paving is called in the trade) no less than 1/8" per foot (the absolute minimum). If stones are particularly rough surfaced, a slope of 1/4" per foot is better. (Incidentally, that is a half a bubble on a 4-ft. level.) More than that, and you may really notice the slope.

Set up lots of stakes around the perimeter. Mark the slope on the stakes by measuring with a builder's level or water level. A patio that is 20 feet deep will be 5" lower at its outer perimeter than it is next to the house. When you're on your knees, it may look like too much slope to accommodate furniture, but it's not.

SELECTING STONE FOR PATIOS

Flatwork should be as smooth as possible, flushing one stone to the other. If the stones aren't flush, the differing heights are called lippage. Tight joints and gauged stone make lippage more of an issue. Super smooth marble dance floors or granite lobbies require machine grinding with diamond impregnated stones for their characteristic slick finish.

Flagstone patios are less demanding, but if the stones aren't flush, a little water won't flow off when it hits the flush joint. No matter how well you slope a patio, if you use natural flagstone some pools will form in the depressions in the stone. (Using gauged flagstone, which is milled on both sides, eliminates this.)

Slate is an inferior material for patios – it tends to stay slick as the slate sheds powdery shale in minuscule amounts. Bluestone is better for outside applications and looks an awful lot like slate.

Most people want big pieces of stone in a patio. A two-person stone looks better, no doubt, but it's a lot harder to place just right on the string and involves lifting and adjusting the bed several times – tapping down and listening for voids, and then moving the strings. Labor rates for paving these days can exceed $10 a square foot plus materials (maybe more for dimensioned stone).

If the patio is to be laid with dimensioned stone or you're planning to drive a vehicle on it, the stone should be set on a poured concrete slab. If the stone is dimensioned, it can be set with thinset (white thinset for limestone, gray for slate). Natural flagstone can be set with mortar.

Some designers prefer raked or depressed joints in flagstone, thinking silt and water will settle in the joints and moss will grow between the stone. Having raked or depressed joints sacrifices a bit of stability and makes the bed wetter. Both things will promote stones popping loose, usually long after the project is finished. Flush joints lock in the stone all around the perimeter and stop almost all movement as well as simplify the flow of runoff.

If a stone does pop after it has been set in a cement bed (either from stepping on the edges before grouting or after the job is finished), it can be repaired by coating the back of the stone with thinset, using a notched trowel. The teeth of the notched trowel should scrape the stone's surface, leaving ribs coated with thinset. A quarter-inch notched trowel used this way will only raise the stone 1/16" or so higher than it was before the repair. If the surrounding joint prevents the stone from being

lifted, the joint may need to be chiseled out or (worst case) the stone may need to be broken. It's too bad when this happens, but making the repair as unnoticeable as possible is the goal. Don't waste time on blame, just concentrate on the repair.

Spreading thinset with a notched trowel on the back of a patio stone that popped up.

A work in process: The patio is laid. The curved fieldstone wall is in place. The coping on the top of the wall and the steps have not been set; a plywood ramp covers the area where the steps will be.

• CUTTING FLAGSTONE BY HAND

My best tip for cutting flagstone is always cut from the corners to the center. Start at one end of the cut and work towards the center, then start at the other end and work towards the center again. Going from left to right and ending your cut on the corner or end of the line will make the last break cut into the main body of the stone.

Flagstone used for paving projects is generally 1" to 1-1/2" thick. A chisel line can be scored on one side and the stone can be flipped over and scored on the other side. Increasing the pressure of each hammer strike will eventually cause the stone to break along the chiseled score. The line can then be cleaned up with a hammer and chisel, or just a hammer. If you're repeatedly unsuccessful with a hammer and chisel, a diamond blade will make the cut quickly and accurately.

• SAWING THINNER FLAGSTONE

Cutting thinner stone for paving with a diamond blade is the most inconspicuous blade-cut to make – the sawn edge will be concealed by the joint (either mortared or filled with soil). For tight curves, use a smaller diameter blade, such as the 4" blade made for grinders and small trim saws.

After the stone is marked for cutting, follow the line with a shallow cut to mark where the line is, then repeat, making the cut deeper with each pass. The groove made by the first shallow cut helps guide the blade as you score deeper.

Laying a hose on the flagstone so that the first score you cut will flood with water will make the cut faster and extend the life of a diamond blade. Having an assistant spray the saw blade with water as you cut is a good makeshift process for making wet cuts.

• SAWING THICKER FLAGSTONE

Sawing thick stone is best done with a bull saw. It is an expensive way to cut stone and should be resorted to after chiseling fails relentlessly. If a cut on flagstone is a very specific shape or the shape is repeated, make a pattern out of craft paper, roofing felt, or a piece of wood. Covering the saw's metal table with masking tape will keep a lighter colored stone from being marked with dark streaks. On more polished or smooth stones, apply the masking tape to the stone itself and mark the cutting line on the tape. (This procedure is used for cutting stone countertops.)

Below: Cutting flagstone with a circular saw.

Above: The centerpiece of this patio is a millstone surrounded by cobblestones. Although now scarce at salvage yards, newly manufactured millstones and cobblestones can be bought at garden centers and landscape materials supply centers.

Right: A stone patio provides the transition between the wooden porch and the garden of this house. The cast concrete bench and planter are ornamental, somewhat formal touches and provide a private place to sit and rest.

Above and right: Smooth, flat stones are ideal for patios intended for furniture, allowing you to create outdoor rooms for relaxing or dining. In shady areas, paving stones set in dirt or sand will eventually become surrounded with moss. The colors of the moss provide a visual transition to the grass and ground cover beyond the patio.

An overhead trellis provides patterned shade on mossy stones set in sand. A canopy of climbing roses lends fragrance and color and deepens the shade, providing contrast with the sunny garden beyond the gate.

Right: Large rectangular stones, uniformly spaced in sand, provide logical geometry on this patio.

GRAVEL & STONE PATIO

Gravel and stone can be combined to create a fast, easy, do-it-yourself patio. The widely spaced stones are set in a base of granite dust, and pea gravel is simply swept into the areas around them as filler. Advantages include:

• The gravel "joints" can be wider and more irregular, so cutting is unnecessary and fitting is minimal.

• The gravel allows the use of a wide variety of stone shapes.

• The gravel provides a permeable surface.

• Only minimal preparation is required.

The stone-and-gravel treatment is most suitable for a patio in a flat area, where runoff and drainage are not a problem.

chapter 13

STONE STEPS

When you climb steps, your body expects them to be at the same height. If a step is a different height, you'll likely trip. For safety, risers (the vertical part) must be the same height and the treads (the horizontal part where you step) should be the same depth. For the same reason, steps shouldn't move.

The need for consistent dimensions of treads and risers are fundamental to the principles of step

design. Even winding or spiral stairs have a path plotted in the wedge shaped treads that steer movements as we ascend or descend in repetitive cycles.

The most comfortable outdoor steps have 14" treads and 6" risers. Interior stairs are generally composed with 12" treads and 7" risers and are accompanied by a handrail for integrated balance. Use these measurements as a basis for plotting your steps.

Right: Stone steps lead down a hill to a patio below. The stone used to pave the landing is the same as the stone on the patio. Low walls on either side of the landing provide a comfortable place to sit. The granite coping, made from the same material as the steps, is dressed (chiseled) on all four sides and has the look of a bench top. See the following pages for illustrations and examples.

CONSIDERATIONS

In choosing the type of steps to build, consider how much and what kind of use they will get. When steps are intended to accommodate a high volume of foot traffic, they must be durable. If steps lead to a shed that will see frequent trips with hands full of tools or from a driveway, the steps must be solid and predictable. Steps that see lighter use and/or have handrails can be less even and still function well.

- Commercial masons typically first pour a set of steps with concrete and then clad them with stones set in a bed of mortar fortified with an acrylic bonding agent. The joints are depressed around the stones to provide gutters for water to flow off the face of the stone tread. (Fig. 1)
- An alternative to using smaller stones set on concrete is the use of stone slabs that are fabricated to the proper dimensions and then set in formed and poured steps with considerations made to their final height above the concrete underlayment. (Fig. 2)
- Steps are usually 3 feet or 4 feet wide (2 feet is a mite cozy). Steps 6 feet wide are luxurious – they will be a gathering spot at garden parties and act as bleachers for revelers. Steps can be abutted with plants and soil, but the functional width will be reduced as the plants grow over the treads. Borders of stone or low walls beside the steps restrain plants and the ever-encroaching dirt that collects in corners and edges. (Fig. 3) Side walls can discreetly house lighting boxes and conduit for the wires that feed them – an added asset.
- Drystacked steps must be shimmed underneath with smaller stones to lift them to the proper height and finessed with gravel to keep the upper stone properly placed. A hidden mortar joint, recessed 1" from the face of the stone, can provide a drystacked look and add permanence.
- Step risers should overlap the lower treads. One stabilizes the other. For a 14" tread, use an 18" stone – it will make a solid bed for the small stone shims that elevate the next slab and act as a dam to hold back the soil, gravel, or cement base beneath the tread slab. The weight of the slab will solidify the riser wall so it needn't be 8" thick, the minimum for structural masonry.
- If smaller stones are used for treads instead of slabs, they must be laid in cement to consolidate them. Mortar frees up the variety of stone sizes you can use to compose a step, and the step can be approached like a tiny wall with a stable coping.
- A step should be level across the front with a slight slope across the depth of the tread of no more than 1/4" per foot to keep water from pooling. Pooling water promotes slick spots, so stones with bowls or depressions that will hold water and can't be tilted enough to shed the water must have a gutter chiseled (or sawn) to spill the water. (Another option is to select a different stone.)
- Steps are often wider at the bottom tread and smaller at the top, giving the illusion of greater ascent and a sweeping motion like water spilling down a hill. This device of classical architecture can be applied to natural stone surrounded by curved retaining walls for an inspiring effect.
- If you want your treads curved out on the sides, make a pattern. Masonite, 1/4" thick, makes an ideal pattern material and can be cut with a jigsaw.
- Stones that pop loose can be fixed with thinset tile cement or epoxy to re-adhere them to the bed after all dust has been removed.

Continued on next page

Stone slab steps. Light boxes were added to the side walls for night safety.

Fig. I

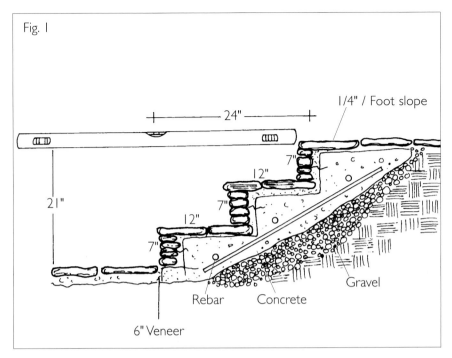

24"

1/4" / Foot slope

7"

12"

7"

21"

12"

7"

Rebar   Concrete   Gravel

6" Veneer

Using a crowbar to level and shim steps.

Fig. 2

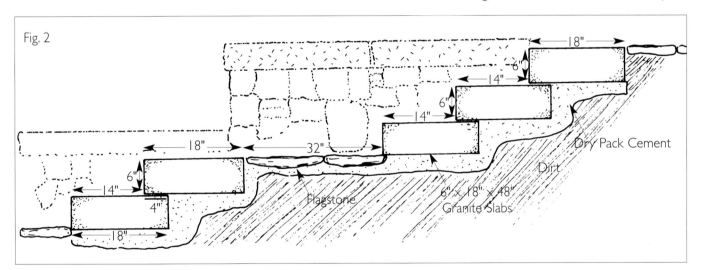

18"

6"

14"

6"

14"

18"

32"

Dry Pack Cement

6"

Dirt

14"

4"

Flagstone

6" x 18" x 48"
Granite Slabs

18"

Fig. 3 – Side Walls
Keep gravel from settling

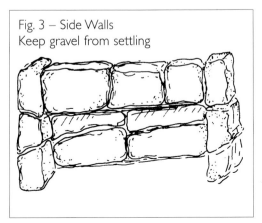

Fig. 4 – Dry Stacked Stone set in pea
gravel or 1-1/2" dry pack

6"

CHOOSING STEP MATERIALS

Heavy stones are less likely to come loose, and full slabs are best. Natural stone slabs are never truly regular in shape, but the steps they can create must be. Rough tread surfaces can be ordered from fabricators specified with combed treads cut with saws or sandblasted finishes. Chisel faced or "pitched faced" risers are more compatible with natural stone walls as part of a stonescape.

Scraps from monument makers make good treads, but their polished (lapidary) finish must be scarred with a chisel or grinder or they will be too slick when they get wet. These free scraps, usually between 6" and 8" thick, can be mortared together side by side. Dressing out the stone with a chisel or a bushing hammer can make them an ideal material.

Cement underlayment for limestone and marble should use white portland cement instead of gray portland. Gray portland will rise through even thick marble and limestone and cause stains. Don't learn this lesson the hard way. The slight difference in price for white portland or white thinset is worth it.

Right: Large irregular stones are set into a slope to form steps. A simple wooden railing provides a visual frame and secure support. Placing the cleave line at the middle of the step allows water to drain. Plants keep soil from washing over the stone.

It all adds up: Irregular stepping stones are used as treads on these steps. Consistent riser height is achieved by carefully measuring the smaller stones underneath the stepping stones and shimming to ensure a good fit.

These granite slab steps with dressed edges are bordered by a wall on one side.

Left: Flush-jointed slate steps lead to a patio. The risers are short and the treads are deep and wide. The larger stones on the edges of the treads were placed so their straight edges would form natural-looking but uniform outer boundaries. Interior areas were filled with smaller stones and cement.

Right: Wide steps from the garden lead to the house above. The subtle curves encourage meandering, and the landings invite the climber to stop and enjoy the views.

Below: A study in contrasts. Recessed joints on the flagstone risers, columns, and wall accentuate the flush joints of the treads and walkway.

chapter 14

Water Features

Ponds, Streams & Waterfalls

Stone and water were meant for each other. The stillness of stone and the movement of water alter sound and light as they collide. Water, whether in a natural stream or a fountain is always coming, always going, always there. The stones lie placidly, indifferent to the destination or the return. Combining the movement of water and the stillness of stone to create a backyard pond or waterfall can be a satisfying expression of your artistry.

Water features are used residentially to please the eye and to mask unwanted sounds of road and air traffic. They provide a delightful destination for birds as well. A waterfall, pond, or fountain can serve as a focal point for an entire project.

Creating a water feature has never been easier for do-it-yourselfers. At one time, you needed the skills of a mason, a plumber, and an electrician to create one, but now plastic tubing and pumps can be found in garden centers and building supply stores as well as in specialty shops that specialize in pond parts and installation.

Infrastructure

A water supply to replenish the pool or pond is a necessary aspect of design, and routing to the pond is an element of design. Planning for a hookup or water line to refill a pond will keep you from having to drag a hose over plantings each time. One nice disguise I saw was a water line leading to a slightly modified old hand pump. Another was nestled in a pile of stones and boulders.

The course of the pipe that serves the pump for streams and waterfalls is also a matter of design. How will it be hidden? If it is buried, the path is important. Some designers feel it is worth the extra trouble and expense to bury copper tubing rather than to use the black plastic pipe that comes with most pond kits.

Right: In this backyard, two ponds are fed by a stream filled with boulders, tumbled stones, and pea gravel. The upper pond is fed by a waterfall; a pump in the lower pond is attached to a pipe that carries water to the waterfall. The ponds and stream are lined with cement.

PONDS WITH VINYL LINERS

A thick polyvinyl membrane is sold as a pond liner to keep water from dissipating into the soil. Great care must be taken in placing the liner so rocks and roots won't tear it. After excavation, the prepared site should be checked for roots and stones by rubbing a bare hand over its entirety. Be sure to clip protruding roots with pruning shears and meticulously remove all the rocks – this is particularly important if the liner is to be covered with stone. Felt matting, available as an underlayment for the vinyl, increases the cost of an installation significantly but can help protect the membrane from tears.

The dirt from the excavation can be used to elevate a sloped area around the pool to divert runoff so it won't contaminate the pool water. The vinyl should overlap the top edges of a pond by approximately 1 foot; covering that edge effectively requires stones that are tightly fitted. Rounded stones called creek rock or river rock are prized for their compatibility with ponds and waterfalls, but trimming them for a tight fit destroys their smooth, rounded lines. Laying stone several layers deep can help conceal the liner and hide pipes, tubing, and conduits for overflow spillways and wires.

Pond with a liner.

A STONE-LINED POND

An attractive way to hide the liner is to dig a shelf around the edge of the pool and create a stone wall that starts a foot or more below the water line. This can be a drystacked wall that leans against the liner and presses back into the soil. The shelf a foot or so below the water line rests on both the soil and the stones lining the pool and makes a smooth visual transition to the water's surface. Extending the liner on a slope provides a base for gravel or stone dust that will absorb water in the pool, creating an area conducive for water-loving plants.

Right: Stones are piled around the edges of the pond to form a border.

Stone-Lined Pond
Sectional Drawing

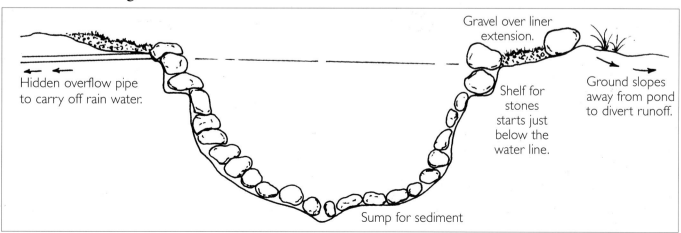

Hidden overflow pipe to carry off rain water.

Gravel over liner extension.

Shelf for stones starts just below the water line.

Ground slopes away from pond to divert runoff.

Sump for sediment

PONDS WITH CEMENT LINERS

Before vinyl liners became available, ponds were lined with cement plastered over expanded metal wire lath, the kind used for stucco. I feel that this mason's approach is still the better way. A cement-lined pond won't puncture or tear, even if the dog gets in it. From time to time, a pond must be cleaned out and the silt and algae removed. If the pond has a stone border placed on the vinyl liner, the stones may shift and pinch a tear if you trudge in it for this routine maintenance. Finding a tear is a nightmare, and removing the stones to find it means doing a hard job all over again. Vinyl deteriorates with age, so disintegration over time is inevitable.

Galvanized or "bright" lath is preferred for ponds over the dark lath used for interior walls of a house. Lath allows for small movements of the soil without cracking the cement and provides a matrix or webbing to consolidate the cement. Wire lath bends and contours well. It is used to make dinosaurs at putt-putt courses and imitation stones at water parks. Familiarizing yourself with this material can begin with a pond. Discovering the possibilities of wire lath and cement can open doors to fabrication with masonry that you may apply as further expressions to your stonescape.

When handling wire lath, **always** wear gloves and long pants. Tripping or losing your balance in a pond is a likely possibility; wire lath makes a nasty scrape and the sharp points on the edges can cause puncture wounds.

A pond made of a wire lath form covered with cement stucco. The exposed pipe – capped off during the cementing process so it won't get clogged up – is for a pump.

To line a pond with lath, begin by digging out the area for the pond. Be sure to provide a channel for silt and debris to settle below the pump. Then line the excavated area with metal lath, overlapping the sections 3-4"; if the edges flip up, secure them with short pieces of tie wire and twist the ends with pliers.

Cementing wire lath is more like plastering or applying stucco than like pouring a footing. Gravel is omitted from the mix for ease in spreading and to avoid bumps. The wheelbarrow batch for a cement-lined pond mix is 10 shovels of sand to 4 shovels of portland. (Resist the temptation to make the mix richer with portland; if you do, it will crack as it cures.)

Add water – how is a matter of preference. Here are the options:
• *Wet like plaster:* Will spread thinly, requiring multiple coats.
• *The consistency of floor mix used by tilesetters:* Will hold in the matrix of the lath, but is difficult to apply vertically on the walls of the pond.
• *Like mortar for stone (my preference):* Will be stiff enough to hold a ball and not squeeze through the fingers.

However you mix it, apply enough coats to reach a thickness of about 1". Let dry between coats, and let the final coat dry.

To assure the pond will be watertight, coat the dry cement with a waterproofing portland-based coating like Damtite, a product commonly used to seal leaky basement foundations. The product comes in colors like brown and aqua blue (dark brown is recommended for reflecting pools; the color helps conceal stains from algae). The tiny fiberglass fibers in the coating interlock, adding strength and filling in any hairline cracks. Manufacturers recommend adding an acrylic bonding agent to the water used to hydrate the mix, which improves adhesion. These types of portland-based coatings are available from swimming pool and fountain supply houses as well as masonry supply stores.

Ponds with Cement Liners (cont.)

WHAT ABOUT FISH?

For many people, having fish is the reason for having a pond. Different fish have different requirements – they may need bio-filters and perhaps a cooling tower for a properly balanced habitat. They may also require chemicals and frequent monitoring. And you have to feed them.

My next door neighbor bought some trout from a fish market for his pond with the same detachment as buying cut flowers. After the weather warmed up, the fish died. (Of course, he was on vacation and the fish were in my care at the time.) Fish in ponds are subject to other natural perils – one couple we visited who have a koi pond told us about the time a mink got into their yard and killed six fish. Two of the fish were worth hundreds of dollars.

Applying a portland-based fiberglass coating to the pond. The color was chosen to match the stones that will be used to border the pond and fill the stream.

MAINTENANCE AND REPAIRS

With fish or not, a pond costs money to build and maintain. Your water bill could increase by as much as 25 percent to replace water lost during evaporation, especially if there is a waterfall. Sometimes the liner leaks, even if it is cemented. (In my experience, usually there is a crack somewhere between the wall that makes the waterfall and the pool above it.) It is a repair that can shut down a pond because water leaking behind a wall will de-stabilize it quickly.)

To fix a leak, find the crack, chisel it out, clean it of all dust, paint it with acrylic bonding agent, and tuck point it with cement. Let it cure for a few days, then start up the pump and check it. Avoid silicone and stick with cement for these kinds of masonry repairs. To repair a vinyl liner, follow the manufacturer's instructions.

STREAMS & WATERFALLS

Streams can be made with cement placed in a furrow dug in the ground. The cement can be hidden with stones and rounded pea gravel of various sizes to create a streambed that realistically mimics a natural creek. The key is to use stones of several sizes that are rounded as they would be in nature. Interspersing plants among the boulders and stones make banks look natural. Long, steep streams will need a water source. Since water can't be recycled and pumped back up a steep hill, the streambed is poured shallow, then filled with the varied stones. Larger water features with streams and ponds incorporate a well especially drilled for the purpose.

It is a matter of taste, of course, but I think waterfalls look best if homage is paid to nature through an attempt at impersonation. A waterfall is a good place to use boulders and slabs, cemented with discreet hidden mortar joints. Pockets for plants (be sure to provide a dry path to reach them) can add a colorful frame to a backyard tableau.

Large slabs for waterfalls and imitation shoals can be obtained from monument companies and at quarries – wherever large cubic stock is sawn into slabs. The outer cleaved edge of the cubic stock is discarded after the cube is sawn into regular slabs and large tapered pieces can be broken into slabs that fit on a pickup truck. The cleaved surface of a cube scrap shifts flowing water into rivulets, and stones placed on the slab can alter the water's course and affect the sound. Japanese gardeners will sweep a rocky shoal to remove algae so the stone can induce this moving shimmer.

Copper tubing at the end of a concrete stream bed.

Two ponds are connected by a waterfall. Water spills down the waterfall from the upper pond to the lower pond. A pump in the lower pond re-circulates the water to the upper pond.

Granite dust covered with creek stones at the edge of a pond makes an inviting habitat for water-loving plants.

Above: A wooden bridge over a stream links stone-paved walkways.

Right: Mix it up! Stones and boulders in a variety of sizes give this stream a natural look.

Right: A raised pond with a stone border provides formal setting that harmonizes with the classical look of the tiered cast iron fountain.

Left: Drystacked thin stone obscures the vinyl liner and provides a whimsical border for this garden pond.

Below: A teak bench near a pond provides a spot for quiet contemplation.

chapter 15

STONE BENCHES

Stone benches are simple to build. They provide a place for you to sit and enjoy your stonescape and – unlike most garden furniture – they don't require maintenance (such as painting or cleaning) and they don't have to be shielded from inclement weather. With properly chosen materials and placement, a bench can be a permanent landscaping feature you will enjoy for years.

Stone slabs for benches are best if they are 3 to 5 feet long and 1 to 2 feet wide. Thick slabs look better to me; a slab less than 2" thick may one day crack. Thicker slabs also offer the stability of a high dead load. (Masons traditionally have relied on weight pushing straight down to stabilize things forever.) You can have slabs cut to your specifications or build your bench from stone pieces crafted by nature.

Right: A poured and stamped concrete walkway provides stable footing in front of a simple stone bench.

How High?

Though people will sit on almost anything outside, I have found that sitting on stonework is better if it is a little higher than a typical dining room chair, which is 17-1/2". My favorite height for a stone bench is 20". With the height in mind, the composition of a stone bench is easy to calculate.

Figuring the Size

If the slab for the stone bench is 5" thick, then the base of the bench should be 15" above the surface and buried 8" – a total of 23". You can fudge a little by digging a hole 8-12" deep and shoveling cement in the hole to adjust the height, and then place the stone legs in the cement. See Fig. 1.

Placing a Bench

1. Dig the holes for the legs.
2. Dress out the tops of the legs, removing any lumps and points so the bench stone will rest without wobbling.
3. Mix some cement. Shovel cement in the holes. Place the legs. Let cure a few hours.
4. Mix some mortar. Apply a pad of mortar to the tops of the legs. A pad of mortar will act as a shim at the top of the legs and help in adjusting the stone slab.
5. Place the stone slab on the legs and compress the edges of mortar by tuckpointing. Use wooden wedges as needed to adjust the bench top. If the stone bench top rests on the legs securely, you can plop down on it right after you finish, but wait a day to sit on the bench if you are using mortar.

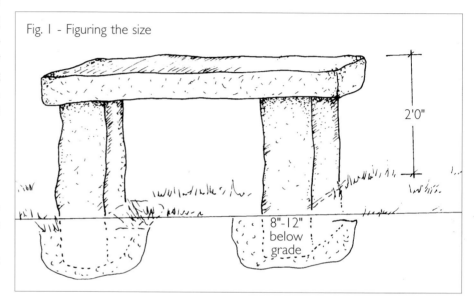

Fig. 1 - Figuring the size

2'0"

8"-12" below grade

FOR FURTHER READING

The Art of the Stone Mason by Ian Cramb (Betterway Books, F&W Publications, Inc., 1992). A great book on masonry as it has been done for centuries by a truly great mason. Technical drawings for arches and turrets that take stonework to the highest level.

The Art and Craft of Stonescaping by David Reed (Lark Books, 1998). Much better than most stone books by landscapers; the focus is on dry stacking stone. Really nice pictures and gentle text.

Moving Heavy Things by Jan Adkins (HMCO, 1980). A small book with perfectly drawn pictures of old jigs and tricks to move just about anything. Wry text.

Stonework by Charles McRaven (Story Publications, 1997). A thorough book of techniques and methods of gathering and setting stone with black and white photos and drawings.

Natural Stonescapes by Richard Dube, APLD, and Frederick C. Campbell (Storey Publications, 1999). An emphasis on oriental theory of stone composition.

METRIC CONVERSION CHART

Inches to Millimeters and Centimeters

INCHES	MM	CM
1/8	3	.3
1/4	6	.6
3/8	10	1.0
1/2	13	1.3
5/8	16	1.6
3/4	19	1.9
7/8	22	2.2
1	25	2.5
1-1/4	32	3.2
1-1/2	38	3.8
1-3/4	44	4.4
2	51	5.1
3	76	7.6
4	102	10.2
5	127	12.7
6	152	15.2
7	178	17.8
8	203	20.3
9	229	22.9
10	254	25.4
11	279	27.9
12	305	30.5

Yards to Meters

YARDS	METERS
1/8	.11
1/4	.23
3/8	.34
1/2	.46
5/8	.57
3/4	.69
7/8	.80
1	.91
2	1.83
3	2.74
4	3.66
5	4.57
6	5.49
7	6.40
8	7.32
9	8.23
10	9.14

INDEX